Suddenly Single Woman's Guide to Surviving Divorce

Learn The Things No One Tells You. Get What You Deserve: Financial Security, Emotional & Physical Stability. Manage Expectations of Family & Friendships. Don't Be Blindsided During The Divorce Process.

Written and Lived by:
Lynda Lighthouse Transier

Copyright © 2016 Lynda Lighthouse Transier
Houston, TX 77019
www.SuddenlySingleWomen.me

Publisher:
Elite Online Publishing
Sandy, UT 84070
www.EliteOnlinePublishing.com

ALL RIGHTS RESERVED. This book contains material protected under International and Federal Copyright Laws and Treaties. Any unauthorized reprint or use of this material is prohibited. No part of this book may be reproduced or transmitted in any form or by any means electronic or mechanical including photocopying, recording, or by any information storage and retrieval system without express written permission from the author/publisher.

ISBN-13: 978-1533121349
ISBN-10: 1533121346

Register this BOOK!

Register your book and you will receive a free "What to ask your attorney" divorce guide along with updates to this book, access to more information, and access to our blog that help you ALONG YOUR JOURNEY.

Just visit: www.SuddenlySingleWomen.info

For more stories, adventures, and advice about the topics covered in this book, I invite you to follow my blog at SuddenlySingleWomen.Wordpress.com.

Dedication

Dedicated to women everywhere who have loved, married, divorced, and worked hard to heal their broken hearts while finding their smiles once again.

Table of Contents

Forward

1- Survival Mode and How You Handle Your Feelings

2- Divorce, Legal Rights and Lawyers

3- Family Issues

4- The Friends

5- Therapy

6- Employment

7- Finances and Budgets for the Present

8- Financial Future

9- Education / Training

10- Home, Your Refuge

11- Fashion on a Budget

12- Fitness and Self-Preservation

13- Outside Interests

14- Faith, Contentment, Inspiration, Spirituality & Motivation

15- Dating

Acknowledgments

Where do I begin to express my most humble gratitude to the many people who have touched my heart and enriched my life through this process?
The first acknowledgment would have to be to my parents: without them, I would not be the person I am today. I offer gratitude to my mother, Katy Lighthouse, who always shows me by example how to be gracious and rise above the fray. My father, Terry Lighthouse (deceased since 1998) who always gave of himself, and taught me to believe in myself, no matter what others might say.

While this was tough on the family, it also was challenging to my many friends who got caught up in the firestorm. Their assistance is varied and ongoing but I could not have made it without any of them, so here goes.

Thanks to Karen Johnson for not leaving me "in the dark," to Debra Bearden for showing up day after day, to Kay and Greg Gregg for offering me a place to stay, to Bonnie Hellums for crucial advice and guidance, to Alexander Rogers and Joe Abuso for the reality check, and to Wendy Burgower for being the best attorney and guiding me through the process.
Many thanks to Don Graubart, Greg Gregg and Barry Galt for feeling like saving my marriage was worth a phone call to my husband. Gratitude goes out to these special women: Patsy Chapman,

Charlotte Strange, Ceci Wallace and Anne Graubart, whose actions are too many to list, but whose insight and empathy started me on my road to recovery.

I appreciate the love and shared adventures over the past thirty years of the Renegades: Lynn Bahm, Gigi Peck, Donna Lewis, Vicki Fisher, Lynne Smith and again Kay Gregg. The support and encouragement for my blog and book comes from my divorce recovery group, including: Sherolyn and Randy Hancock, Katie O'Harra, Erica Zack, Margarita Longoria and Carol Cox.

Thank you to Jenn Foster and Melanie Johnson, publishers with Elite Online Publishing, and David Smith, editor, for believing in me, believing in my story, and keeping me in the correct "person and tense" since to me, "first person, second person and third person" has nothing to do with grammar and everything to do with being in a line!

Forward

In the spring of 1980 I was a teacher in Spring Branch Independent School District. Pregnant with my first child, I was sharing the crazy ups and downs of pregnancy with fellow teacher and first time mom-to-be Glenna. We made a pact, a vow if you will, that whoever delivered first would tell the other everything to expect about labor and delivery—no gory detail left out. It was our attempt to overcome the fear of the unknown. If you know what's coming, you can prepare yourself, at least to a degree. If you can plan ahead, you won't feel blindsided.

With childbirth, I discovered, it worked. Sort of.

Looking back, that's how I had to handle it. You see, I'm a planner, an organizer, a type-A personality. I fought it for years, but it always seemed to win. Finally I gave up, made peace with it, and discovered it was my friend after all. It was a friend that wanted to protect me from what I didn't know was coming.

But sometimes you can't plan for what's coming. Sometimes something is around the corner that will change all your plans, your dreams, your hopes, your life. My "something" arrived in 2001. And no, it wasn't 9/11.

It's been said that how you handle what's thrown at you makes you the person that you are. I always wanted to be the person who handled things with integrity—a good person who did the right things and followed the rules. I was the good daughter, the good wife, the good mother, the kind of person my parents had brought me up to be. I was proud of the job I was doing and the person I had become. That was about to be severely tested.

In December 2001, my husband and I were celebrating our 25th wedding anniversary. The evening started when we renewed our vows in the church chapel with our pastor, surrounded by our two adult sons and six very special long-time friends. After we left the church, we all headed to the country club for a dinner dance with two hundred family members and friends from the past twenty-five years.

At the party, I surprised my husband with a custom-built Harley Davidson motorcycle, something he had always wanted. Buying a Harley under the radar was not an easy task to accomplish, since he was a CPA and Chief Financial Officer who handled *all* the family finances. However, my sons and I pulled it off. After all, why let the "middle-aged crazies" set in for my husband when I could provide a motorcycle for him myself? Life was beautiful. We were living the American Dream. I felt like I was in the middle of a twenty-first century version of *Leave It To Beaver, Father Knows Best,* or *Ozzie & Harriett.*

Five months later all my dreams and plans for the rest of my life came crashing down around me. We had renewed our vows in front of God, church, family and friends. Those vows had been broken.

When the truth came out, I was crushed beyond belief. You are never prepared for that kind of betrayal, never. But the personal details of that betrayal and broken promises are *not* why I wrote this book.

Flash forward to February 2007 when he filed for divorce and it was three weeks before I found out. Talk about being overwhelmed with the fear of the unknown. Suddenly I was in survival mode, like treading water in the deep end of the pool with muscle cramps. I had no idea where I was heading.

The next phase of my life was extremely difficult. As with childbirth, there was no way to avoid it. But my friend Glenna and I had had a good plan while we were pregnant in 1980. Being informed about the process didn't alleviate the pain, but it was a big help.

If you are going through a divorce, or have just gone through one, nothing can immediately take away the pain. (Well, maybe George Clooney calling, but I think he's taken.) What every woman who finds herself in this situation desperately needs is to know the answers to the questions she has. And, maybe more important, to know what questions to have. In my experience, *not knowing what I didn't know* was what blindsided me.

Looking back, I had a lot of friends, usually well-meaning, who were glad to give me advice and to tell me what I should or should not be feeling (*not* particularly helpful). What I really needed, however, was one who had been through the process herself, who knew the ropes by experience, and who was willing to sit down with me over a cup of coffee and say, "I know this is horrible. But let's level-headedly go through everything you're going to need to know to make it through this. You're going to make it."

That's what I want to be through this book—a good friend who will do everything she can to help you through. You and I are sitting at Starbucks. I've ordered a hot chai latte. You've ordered ... whatever it is you order! I listen empathetically as you relate the latest horrible things you are having to endure. And then I finally get around to saying, "OK, let's talk about what you're going to need to know to avoid the giant potholes waiting around the corner."

Because the potholes are out there, waiting for you to fall in. They don't care that you're in pain and don't want to think about them. But armed with some advance knowledge, you *can* navigate around them. You *can* make it through easier. And you *can* come out on the other side in better shape than, right now, you can ever imagine.

As we chat at Starbucks, I'll rely on help from some wonderful, thoughtful and caring professionals who entered my life at this stage and helped me endure. I will use examples of what I went through, and what others have gone through, to help you understand the process. The examples will help guide you through some tough decisions you will have to make. Substitute names or initials will be used to protect the identities of most of the people in the book. Like a real conversation, the book will go from one topic (chapter) to another, but also like a real conversation, many of the topics will be intertwined.

Most important, this conversation will be from the heart, with the hope that you will come through this awful experience and find yourself a whole person on the other side. Let me be clear about one thing: I write this from the point of view of the woman who did *not* want the divorce. In no way do I represent myself to be an attorney, a counselor, a psychiatrist, or a therapist. I'm a woman who went through a life-altering experience, learned a lot, and wants to help other women who are about to face it, or who have already faced it but are still stuck in misery.

My gift to you is that while you didn't deserve what happened to you, you will be a better person for it. You *will* survive and you *will* smile again. I wish you blessings and all good things to come your way.

Godspeed,

Lynda Lighthouse Transier

1- Survival Mode and How You Handle Your Feelings

Going through the divorce process, I never could quite understand one thing: how many people tell you how and what you should be feeling. Usually these are people who have never themselves experienced separation, adultery, or divorce, and now they're telling you how you should feel? Seriously?

Your feelings are *your* feelings. They are no one else's.

See blog post:

http://suddenlysinglewomen.me/2013/07/15/validation-we-all-need-it/

Be prepared. Everyone has an opinion and advice they want to give you. Want it or not, you're going to get it. My favorite was what a previously close friend of mine, we'll call her Clara, shared in a group of mutual friends. She didn't understand, she told them, why I couldn't "just get over it?" As if a snap of the finger, a blink of an eye, and everything goes back to normal—there's just no husband now.

Let's be very clear about divorce: no matter why the divorce occurred, things will never go back to normal—whatever you thought normal is or was. That may be a hard pill to swallow, but denying the truth doesn't make things easier. It makes them harder.

Whether you filed for divorce or your spouse did, the reality is that life will never be the same again. It can be *good* again, but it won't be the same. The changes can be as small as returning to your maiden name, or as large as relocation, but your life has changed. You can't go back to the way things were. I tried. I looked for balance, for normalcy, for steady footing. But the divorce process is like riding the ocean waves during a hurricane. For the time being, steadiness is a thing of the past.

So family offers you advice, friends offer you advice, and your soon to be "ex" might even weigh in on what you should be doing and how you should be handling your life. Have you ever come out of a loud rock and roll concert and your ears are ringing and the sensation doesn't go away for a while? The advice doesn't go away, either. Everyone has an opinion, mostly well meaning, but at the end of the day the only person who knows your feelings . . . is *you!*

The speed with which your feelings can be openly expressed, understood, and dealt with is not going to be the same as anyone else's. Professionals can offer guidelines and help, but dealing with your feelings is still up to you.

See blog post:

http://suddenlysinglewomen.me/2013/05/29/words-of-wisdom-from-a-tv-show/

I'm the type A planner and organizer, remember? After my first son was born, I read baby books and listened to advice from friends about when my newborn would sleep through the night. I patiently waited for that week to arrive. I was a walking zombie, and all I longed for was a string of six consecutive hours of sleep. Well, that magic week came and went without so much as a three-hour nap from son #1.

Just as no one can predict your child's first full night of sleep, no one can tell you when the dark gloominess of divorce trauma is going to end. I kept trying to say to friends, "I'm doing the best that I can!" But everyone wants you to hurry up and be "normal" again.

Many therapists liken divorce to a death, and it is a loss: of a way of life, of an intact family, of a love you once had, and, often, of a financial lifestyle. There are, perhaps, worse possible losses in life. I have a beloved friend who lost her daughter, and I'm not saying my loss was as devastating as hers. But it was devastating enough, and so is yours.

What I'm giving you permission to do is acknowledge that what you're experiencing feels like a death. Your marriage is dead. The way your heart is broken cannot just be changed because it's inconvenient for others, or an annoyance to those who surround you. You can't change the way you feel just to please others. The heartache and the fear of the unknown are lodged in your psyche. You didn't ask that they be put there, you weren't given any time to prepare for them, and you can't just wish them away because someone would like you to.

So how do you deal with your feelings?

Let's agree that we are all individuals and there is no one right way to handle your emotions. If you take twelve months to reach some sense of stability, you take twelve months. If you take five years, you take five years. It's not a football game where one can keep score. Don't even try to compare yourself to how others have coped, or how you expect yourself to cope. Your process will simply be your process.

See blog post:

http://suddenlysinglewomen.me/2012/03/06/moving-on-down-the-road-is/

In my experience, everyone experiences loss in divorce. You lose your stable, comfortable future that you had planned and worked hard for. I lost people who I thought were lifelong friends. Your children lose their "two parent" household. There are no winners.

Losses take time to recover from. For me, I became so tired of people saying two little words that I learned to hate: "Move on." "You'll feel better when you move on." "You'll be happier when you move on." "You can start all over when you move on." Didn't people realize that's what I wanted to do? I just wanted it all to be over—the pain, the shame, the hurt, the embarrassment. I wanted to scream, "I'm moving as fast as I can!"

But we aren't like recipes for which you collect all the ingredients, mix them together, bake for an hour, and then serve. We just aren't constructed that way.

Getting someone to move on from their divorce is a bit like trying to get a baby to stop crying when you have no idea what's wrong with her. Like a frustrated parent with the crying baby, your friends don't know what to do to help, so they offer what seem to be logical ways for you to think, or feel, or act. Sometimes it actually is logical; sometimes it's not. The best friends are those who are willing to be patient and stick with you, regardless of how long your process takes.

The ways women deal with divorce are as varied as women themselves, but in my observations, most women fall into one of four approaches. I'll describe them below. Each of these approaches can be a path to healing. As we discuss them, I'd like you to remember this: for your heart to heal, you will finally have to let go of your anger and bitterness. That may seem impossible right now, but it will become necessary. My friend C.W. wrote:

> Anger and bitterness are powerful forces. They only hurt the one holding onto them. I cannot/could not move forward and live my new life unless I let it go. Let all that my ex-husband did/does to me GO! I still have to remind myself almost daily to do so. And he still throws me curve balls.
>
> God, grant me the serenity to accept the things I cannot change, the courage to change the things that I can, and the wisdom to know the difference. This is my mantra.

That's the direction we will have to move toward. How we get there presents various options.

See blog post:

http://suddenlysinglewomen.me/2013/04/01/when-better-isnt-bitter/

The Moving Truck

Some women chose to take this approach. They're strong, they're committed and they're determined. It's not that they're unable to deal with the anger, the hurt, and the disillusionment of the marriage they thought they had. It's that they just cannot, or will not, do it now.

Don't get me wrong, this is not procrastination; it's a form of self-preservation. They step away and watch the moving truck roll down that street where their life used to be.

We've all moved before. You gingerly pack up those breakables, double wrap them in bubble wrap and put them in a sturdy box. Our anger goes into one box, fold that lid down and zip that tape across the top—good and tight. Next you pack the heart. Already broken and shattered into tiny pieces, you scoop up the pieces and carefully put them in a pouch to be worried about later. Box it, and *zip* goes the tape. Next comes the ten, twenty, thirty years of memories, or however many years you were a "couple." These will require the larger wardrobe boxes.

You (figuratively) put the wedding album and the bridal portrait up (did I really wear my hair like that?). You go into your memory storage closet and pull out the hangers full of that first job, first raise, first promotion, first tiny do-it-yourself fixer-upper home. These hangers have lasted a long time because you were the one there since the beginning when, as a couple, you had nothing. You were your husband's support team and the good listener about everything "unfair." Yes, don't forget that cheerleader costume you always wore when he needed a pep talk, encouragement, an "atta boy."

Grab more of those strong hangers to hang in that box of memories all those vacations you couldn't afford but took, the first time the big boss acknowledged you by name around your peers or you were invited to be a table guest at a big time event. Don't forget those "first born" memories, when you shared the news of pregnancy, when you couldn't decide on a girl's name but you already knew what university she was going to attend. By now you need to construct a second wardrobe-size moving box because you can't forget the first tooth, first steps, first day of school, first dance recital, piano recital, t-ball home run or soccer goal.

Slide those bulky hangers over to make room for the family vacation memory albums, family holiday occasions or birthday parties, end of the season trophies. Whew, you didn't know you'd kept so many did you? But then you're the only one packing up the memories of this family because he didn't care to save any of them on his way out the door.

The next job of packing deals with all those dreams

you shared together. You know the ones. The "what we're going to do after the kids are grown and gone" plans. How many of these you have to pack up probably depends on your relationship and, in part, on its length. Men leave at different times during their marriage, but you still had some "happily ever after, till death us do part" dreams you two shared. These are perhaps the most gingerly packed away, because for some unknown, bizarre reason, you still want to hold on to those.

Even though he took those dreams to the trash dumpster on the way out the door, you just can't quite let go yet. Perhaps you fold over the lids of these boxes without sealing the tape just yet. Those will be the last things placed on the moving truck.

You realize as that moving truck pulls away that eventually you're going to have to see those boxes again. You'll rip them open one by one and deal with those items. Just not now. Because you're strong, you're committed, and you're determined, you'll get to it later.

See blog post:

http://suddenlysinglewomen.me/2012/02/20/73/

The Firing Range

These are the women who decide that the best way to deal with the hurt and the anger is to put their ex on a target at the firing range and unload a full round of ammunition. Forgive me here, but these women just want to blow the hell out of those targets. This makes them feel better. The firing range woman takes her anger out on the man who has ripped her heart to shreds. After all, doesn't everyone tell you to "move on," get rid of all that anger? You don't need to box those feelings up for the moving truck because after you're done with those memories, and those worthless promises, it's going to take a super suction vacuum to suck up all the remains.

You want to vent steam like a teapot, you want to throw things, stomp the stuffing out of them. I had offers from friends to let the air out of all four of his tires. (I declined; I am *not* advocating violence here, but simply acknowledging the need to do *something* with your feelings.) One friend put a tracking device on *her* husband's car, and even though she already knew who he was with, he was no longer able to deny it as he had previously.

Then there was the friend that bought a stuffed toy for the dog. It was male doll and had the word EX in big bold letters on the front. After a couple of days of doggy's teething and chewing, most of it was shredded. However, it was still together enough to hang on the bulletin board in the office to provide the occasional laugh!

You're getting the picture. The anger you feel makes you want to destroy something. Be sure to wear some earplugs at that firing range—it's going to get mighty loud.

The Water Fountain

These women are so crushed that all they can do is cry. They can't believe they've been left after all the things they've done for him. They ask themselves, "This is my reward?" The first night they're left alone in the marriage bed the tears flow so much that by morning their eyes are red, swollen and puffy. These wives walk around the house and everything they look at brings back memories that cause them to cry more. Some think unthinkable thoughts of taking their life; a jar of pills will do it easy, right?

Friends come to comfort you but you're inconsolable. All you do is cry. "Let's get out of the house," they say, but you can barely put one foot in front of another, much less get out of your comfy security blanket bathrobe. You wish you owned stock in a company that makes boxed tissues because you're emptying one every six hours.

Someone finally drags you out of the house for lunch, but all you focus on is the "last" time "he" was here with you. You go clothes shopping, but you hate everything you look at because you're convinced you'll never have another special occasion to attend, anyway.

You cry at billboards showing lovers, at toddlers in the park, at dogs being walked in the evening by a couple holding hands, at the dry cleaners you finally found that would starch his shirt collars just right, at the frozen yogurt store that provided treats for the two of you every Sunday night. Everywhere you go are reminders of the life you used to share, now gone or being shared with someone else in his life.

You cry in church, you cry at doctor appointments, you cry when your flight is delayed and everyone else pulls out their cell phones to alert someone that they'll be late and you have no one to call. You cry when your children look at you in bewilderment wondering how their father could just leave and break up the family unit. You wish you could answer but you are just as baffled as they are.

Get ready for the holidays; they are the worst. The holiday cards won't have the family photo this year that everyone looked forward to seeing. I used my Christmas card as a change of address / change of situation announcement where I announced my new life. Everyone tiptoes around you because they don't want to water log their shoes! You're life is falling apart and they're wondering should they build another ark?

The Round Table Discussion

Many women are so dumbfounded by what has happened to them that they simply want answers. Surely someone they know can help them figure it all out.

"Do you think he'll come back?" "How could he just walk away after all those years?" "Did he ever really love me or was getting married just the thing to do?" "Was I just a surrogate so he could have children?" "Am I going to have to sell my house, get a job, move home?"

You were always led to believe that intelligent people ask questions. Remember my pledge with my fellow pregnant teacher? We asked questions, we needed answers. We needed to understand and be prepared. You're rarely given any warning that your man is leaving. When he does all you're left with are these unanswered questions such as, "Why me?" "What is it that he wants?" "Who is he with?" "What do I do now?"

Your life has suddenly become one giant unanswered question and to anyone and everyone who will listen, you ask what they think. Some will tell you, some will decline, some will even lie to you, believing it's what you want to hear them say or that they're doing the right thing.

You seek counsel from family, friends, your pastor, your therapist, whomever. Eventually they weary of your quest for answers (well, not your therapist; you're paying him or her). I really believe people would give the answers you so desperately seek if they had them. Perhaps even your spouse cannot really answer why he left.

The thing is most men compartmentalize their lives. They often are not even able to answer the "why" questions themselves. When they're at work that's all they think about: business, the next deal, their next proposal, their next raise or bonus, the next merger or acquisition. When they're on the golf course, it's all about the game; they can recall almost every swing, putt, and score on every hole on that course. However, they can't explain to you why they're leaving you. When they walk out, for whatever reason, they have closed the door on that compartment in their life, and most likely will not be coming back through it again.

That doesn't mean it's fair and doesn't mean it's right; it's just the way it is. You have so many unanswered questions that you need answers for before you can move on and we all know how they hate questions.

You're becoming a nag in his mind, so you do the next closest thing and ask his best friends, his family, his siblings, his golf buddies, his running partner, his hunting group, his tennis partner — anyone who spends time with him. You want to know, "What has he told you?" "What's going on in his head?" Be ready to walk away from your Round Table with no more answers to your "Why?" questions than you had when first you sat down. "But how can I move on without answers?" you ask. You search for closure. It's like you're a prosecutor but the defendant is too guilty or too disinterested to even bother taking the stand.

The best advice? Accept that you'll never have the answers and *move on*.

I know that this view of how you feel is simplistic,

or maybe even a bit harsh. The further you get away from the event, the easier it will become to deal with it. Denial only puts off the inevitable, anger only ends up hurting you because he's already made his decision. Crying may cleanse your soul but it only makes him run faster and further. If you ever do find all your answers will it even change anything? Maybe, maybe not, but in the long run, those answers won't bring him back, either. I've seen recovered marriages. I've been counseled by women who got their man back, so it certainly is possible. If it happens to you, you're one of the relatively few lucky ones and I pray you can make it work.

Always remember, however, that your feelings are your own. They don't have to be right or wrong, and people don't have to agree or disagree. Your feelings are yours; you own them. You are not crazy, you are not mean. Everyone else's opinion is just that, an opinion. File it away and consider it only when you are ready or able to. People who offer their opinions and advice mean well, but they are not you. You are unique, you are special and you will get through this.

Looking around at those couples who have made it, who have a real marriage, you might start to become skeptical and think it's all an act. Maybe there's no such thing as happily ever after. You look at the new woman in your ex's life and feel a pang of envy.

Why is she better than me? Why couldn't he still love me? As Professor John Portman, author of *When Bad Things Happen to Other People*, says, you should enjoy schaden-freude. "It hurts to be jealous of people who are wealthier or more beautiful than you are, but schaden-freude—the pleasure you get from the misfortune of someone else—can feel great. You're not rejoicing that these people are suffering, but rather that the karmic system works. We all want to believe that what goes around comes around."

Believe me, what goes around *will* come around, eventually.

2- Divorce, Legal Rights and Lawyers

Preparing for Divorce

There's a line in a Country & Western song that says we're going through the "Big D and I don't mean Dallas." During what part of your wedding day did it ever occur to you that one day you would find yourself here? It never occurred to me; I was so excited to take that next big step in my life's journey.

See blog post:

http://suddenlysinglewomen.me/2012/02/20/72/

We all think we've found that great lifelong partner that we will grow old with, as was the case with most of our parents. No one tells you that when you get to our age you become part of the statistic that almost half of all marriages are now ending in divorce. So what happens after that wedding day? Every case is different, and there are many different reasons for divorce, but all that matters now is how you are going to survive it, and get a fair settlement in the process.

Divorce is never easy; it's the end of your life as you have known it. I don't mean it's literal death, of course, but it is the death of a relationship. Whoever coined the phrase "amicable divorce" never met anyone I know who has gone through the process. I have yet to meet a couple whose divorce was amicable. Have you?

I hope to pass along some thoughts on how to cope with the process, and how to avoid feeling like you are the victim of emotional abuse in the midst of the process. I know, it's almost a given that you feel emotionally abused by the process of getting here; we just don't want that added to. If your husband wants the divorce, he will seek counsel, possibly hire an attorney, all the while telling you "you won't need one" and that you should not seek counsel. Yes you should, yes you do. Protect yourself.

Women wrongly hope that since he was the one who wanted the divorce, and since he has (more than likely) already moved on with someone else, he would want to get the divorce over with quickly. You would be wrong.

You might also think that there would be no ugliness aimed toward you, the mother of his children, his partner in life and the injured party. You would be wrong. Divorce is ugly, pure and simple, and it's an hourly billing rate for the attorneys, so why should it move along quickly? I know with these words I will anger some divorce attorneys, but so be it. There are no simple, "turnkey" divorces. Unless you have been married a relatively brief time with no children (in that case, divorce can be fairly simple), there will be many details to be ironed out, court hearings, separation of property—it goes on and on.

If you think that you are getting to that stage then let me offer a few pointers, generously offered by my wonderful (and experienced) friends.

Cash is King

My attorney once told me "cash is king." Settlements of mostly cash are generally preferred, but that's not the cash I'm referring to here. If you came from, or are coming from, a marriage where all finances are handled by your husband (or, really, even if you are not) you will need to protect yourself early on.

Start taking some amount of cash every week and putting it away in a safe, secure place. I'm not suggesting emptying your checking account. I'm merely saying if you use a debit card at the grocery store where almost all offer a "cash back" option, use it.

If you normally get your cash from an ATM every week or two, raise the amount that you normally take out and hoard some away. Some men might resort to controlling tactics to force you to depend on them, such as making you accept a settlement that is less than fair by stopping their financial support. If you get cut off financially, you will need some cash available to draw upon. Many states have laws to protect you and your lifestyle while going through the divorce process, but unless you and your attorney can get the offending party and his enabling attorney in front of a judge for a hearing, then he can cut you off.

Once the court issues temporary orders, you will feel secure that there is a court order in place that states clearly that he must continue to support you in the same way as when you were living together as husband and wife. Not doing so would put him in contempt of that court order. Guess what? It takes so long to get back in front of that judge that you can become frightened and desperate and might make bad decisions, just to get it over with. Even though court orders prevent acts like this, it happens all the time.

It's not a bad idea, for example, to put a hundred dollars or so away any time you get the chance. Keep it in a safety deposit box. If you have your credit cards cancelled, or the normal support checks stop being deposited in your bank account, you will have a reserve to live on. Many forms of intimidation might come your direction if you refuse to accept their less than fair settlement offer.

Yes, it is against the court orders. Yes, his attorney might try to stall your attempts to get in front of a judge. Yes, you will have moments of desperation. Family and friends will beg you to take the settlement offer to end the mess. You must be strong and hold out for what is rightfully yours. It is what you deserve after those many years of marriage.

If you have not worked outside the home in a long while, your husband might claim you added no value to the bottom line. When that paycheck only has one name on it, that person suddenly thinks it's all his and you deserve very little of it. *You* become the greedy one. We're talked about in the club locker room, we're bashed at his office, we're suddenly the "greedy bitches" trying to take away all the worldly goods that they worked so hard for. Who do we think we are? Stay strong and stand your ground. You did work hard (whether paid or not), you did earn it, and you deserve your fair share.

Credit—The American Way

Here's an essential. If you don't already have it, apply for a credit card in your name. If you've never had any credit established in your own name, it's time. You're going to have to start being responsible for your own life and financial well-being. Your own credit will take some time to establish, but you need to have it no matter your age.

If you know a banker you can talk to, have he or she advise you on how to begin. Apply for a credit card in your name but don't necessarily go out there and use it for things you don't need. It is credit, after all, and must be paid back! Carry a small balance and make timely payments. I had no job and had not worked in years, but I was able to secure a card.

Perhaps you borrow a small sum of money and pay the balance back over a six-month period to establish a good payment record and accountability. It's easier for women these days, but if you get turned down don't panic. Certainly don't go out and apply for five to ten credit cards because all applications are reported to the credit bureaus. Keep it small and keep it simple.

Financial Records

If you've been filing a joint tax return, try to gather three to five years worth of returns and make copies. If you have investment accounts, bank accounts, or retirement accounts, make copies of those statements as well. Hopefully you have access to all those documents, in paper or online. You might be shocked to discover that your name is not listed as a joint holder on any investment or credit accounts, save the one that you might pay the household accounts out of. These is a paper trail, find it.

If your name is not listed on an account, no matter that you are the spouse, they will not send you a copy of a statement, they will not answer any questions, and they certainly will not give you any proceeds out of those accounts. Don't make a blind assumption that you are a signatory on any account just because you trusted that your spouse was taking care of you, and always would.

Separate Property—"Yours, Mine and Ours"!

Start making an inventory of your property, the assets that you know of, and anything of value you may have had before your marriage or received from family as separate property during those years of marriage. My attorney provided me with a valuable worksheet for this at our first meeting. You think you didn't bring anything of substantial value to the marriage, but you'd be surprised.

If you married later in life, chances are you brought things into the marriage that you would want to have awarded to you aside from settlements or property division. Their relative value should not be held against you. The more proof you have though, the better.

When you divorce, the "ours" dissolves more quickly than you can blink an eye. It becomes a battle over "his" and "yours."

Shopping For An Attorney

Getting a divorce as a legal process has little to do with truth or justice. It's the dissolution of a relationship with a division of property, assets, and, possibly, future income streams. It's handled like a business deal; it's just that cold. The love you once shared, the vows you took for richer or poorer, for better or for worse, have led you to the "worse" part.

You need to find an attorney that has your best interest at heart and is willing to go to the mat for you. They all know each other; they spout ugliness at each other over the phone, and then meet for drinks later. You wonder, how can he/she be such good buddies with that awful person representing your soon to be "ex"?

Good question. It's hard to swallow that all the ugliness between the opposing counselors is just part of the process. It's your life, it's your future, but to them you're just another case to settle. It's a game of numbers. I know what you're thinking, but I do not hate attorneys. For the most part, I respect people who represent the law, but somehow a divorce case just brings out the harder, nastier side of some of them.

Start by getting recommendations from friends or family members who have been through this process. You're going to be spending a lot of time with this person so it needs to be someone you can trust, who understands your needs. Do not, I repeat, do not hire someone because he has the reputation of being the premiere divorce attorney in town. Have you checked their fee schedule? In my case I knew I did not want a male attorney. My lack of trust in men, after living through the lies, and deceptions, just did not allow me to consider hiring one.

I wanted someone that could feel the pain I was feeling and would do their best to protect me. Interview as many as you feel is necessary to find the right match. When you meet with them, assess if they "get you." Do they offer you a plan? Is their timetable realistic? What about the fee structure? How much is their retainer? Do they represent more women than men, or vice versa? Are they close to you in driving distance? Is their caseload such that you're a client or just a number to call back later? You'll know if there is a connection, so listen to your instincts.

Your husband might be motivated to get your

divorce over with so he can be with his girlfriend "publicly." He might say he will be fair and equitable, and that you don't need to waste time and money on attorney's fees. Being gullible, and still in shock that it has come to divorce after promises of "I want to make this work," you might be tempted to do as told. If you're still thinking "this isn't really happening to me", you might not seek counsel. Please do.

Your spouse might move out for some "time to be alone and think," he might tell everyone you are working on your issues. While he might say he doesn't want a divorce, he most likely will have already contacted an attorney. If you live in a large city, there are certain attorneys that you hear about, who will represent their client "well" to the detriment of the other spouse. Don't be surprised if he went directly to one of those big name divorce attorneys in your city.

Unbeknownst to you, things could already be set in motion. There you are, hoping for reconciliation, and all the while he is already coming up with the "mine" and "yours." I was blindsided. Don't be like me; you have legal rights and you need to find out what those are.

Texas, where I live, is a "no fault" state. It doesn't

matter the reasons husbands leave, but the flip side to the "no fault" is that it is a community property state. Supposedly, you get half of the assets when you split up and each go on your merry way. Do some due diligence to find out the laws, and your rights in your state.

LG shared her example:

"I'll never forget being in a committee meeting for one of the larger non-profits I volunteered for. Two of my good friends, who happen to be male, and whom I had known for years, came over to see how I was holding up with the separation. They asked me what attorney I had hired, or consulted, and I honestly answered that I had not done that because my husband had told me not to, we would handle this ourselves. Very politely they told me I was being a fool and were sure that my husband had already done so. I told them naively that he had promised not to. They reminded me that I needed to open my eyes.

I had to admit that they made a good point. Both of these men told me to call one particular divorce attorney in town that they knew would be tough and aggressive and would take care of me. If I didn't call him quickly, they would on my behalf. They begged me to be proactive and start taking care of myself.

The next day was Friday, and as I had committed to them, I made the call to the man's office.

I left my name, phone number and the reason for my call. Not, as you would surmise, that I needed divorce advice, but that I was separated with my home on the market, and needed to know what my legal rights were to the proceeds should my home sell? Where would I live? And, more importantly, how would I pay for it?

Imagine my surprise when neither the attorney, nor anyone on his staff, had the courtesy to call me back. Further imagine my shock when a very angry husband called me the following Monday afternoon accusing me of breaking *my* promise to not speak to an attorney? By now you've surely realized as I did that there was only one way he could have known that. He had already contacted the aggressive attorney on his own behalf.

Why, you ask, was I still so gullible, so trusting and so convinced that he would do the right thing? And why had the attorney I called not had the courtesy to return my call, or had someone in his office call instead of leaving me hanging? You'll never understand the actions, but for your own sake you must be prepared for what is about to run you over."

Take the referrals from your friends and set up interview appointments with these divorce specialists. When you're ill, you see a doctor who is a specialist; don't pick this time in your life to go with cheap or inexpensive. I picked three women to interview; I felt strongly that I needed a woman's point of view on the broken wedding vows, etc. The males I had been referred to had only lived up to all expectations of callousness and shallowness. If you know who your husband has hired, find someone who knows and understands his attorney's tactics. At these interviews it is normal to be given paperwork to fill out and basic questions to answer, and you will pay a consultation fee. That really surprised me.

Naïve, I know, but even though they ranged in price, you need to be ready. Most will require a retainer to take the case on, depending on the difficulty they perceive of the future settlement. The more you have in the way of assets, or things to be contested, the longer it will likely take to come to an agreement.

Most cases don't actually end up in court. Judges prefer that you settle your case via your attorneys or through mediation with an impartial "go between." Don't kid yourself: the judges know most of the divorce attorneys on a first name basis outside the courthouse, and the mediators sure do since many of them are former judges or former family law attorneys themselves.

Once you find an attorney that you feel comfortable with, you'll sign a contract for him or her to represent you. Let the games begin, or should I say to batten down the hatches? In a community property state, there is little attention, if any, paid to the cause of the divorce. You have now become a business liability to your spouse. He and his attorney will work hard to put you and your marriage of ten, twenty, thirty or more years into a box, shut close the lid and mark it "case closed."

There are no more "remember the good times"; to your husband the good times are now ahead of him. Whether there was another woman in his life already or not, he's ready to explore. One marriage therapist counsels that "most men don't leave their wives, their children, their families. There is a history with them that cannot be replaced with a fling." But, he added, "Those who do leave almost always have someone in place already, waiting in the wings." Men, he said, don't do "alone."

You need to hire an attorney that will be your advocate. He or she needs to be accessible to you when you have your meltdowns, when your husband pushes your buttons or his attorney attacks your character. You must steel yourself against the onslaught of nastiness that his attorney is going to throw at you. It is unbelievable that they stoop that low.

They'll write nasty letters accusing you of things; your fax machine or email inbox will become your nightmare. The communications become so mean-spirited. You won't believe such anger exists, and is targeted toward you..

Like I said, it gets ugly. If you've only been married a short time, or have no children together, it could be something else. Otherwise, your spending habits, your hobbies, your friends, your housekeeping skills, your weight, your social behavior—the list is endless and all will come under scrutiny and ridicule.

Have your attorney be brutally honest with you about the best case / worst case scenario. What is important to you to walk away with? You'll be sentimental (it's hard not to be), but don't think the opposing side will be. I use the word "opposing" here because when it come to a property settlement, you will feel like the man you once committed to love and honor for the rest of your life has become the opposition. There is no 50/50. There is a "need to win at all costs" feeling that casts a shadow on all negotiations.

Many women cannot quite grasp how the person who wanted the divorce, who filed for the divorce -perhaps without even telling them, and who had already moved on with his affections, could make actually getting the divorce so darn difficult. They think some bit of guilt would make him just do the right thing, take care of them and move on, wouldn't he?

Heaven help you if your family, children, or friends get involved. Marriage is between two people; try to leave the divorce that way, too, as much as you can.

See blog post:

http://suddenlysinglewomen.me/2012/03/14/dragging-the-anchor/

I've heard from so many women who have gone through the divorce process. They share things such as:

"My In-laws were in total denial that my husband had repeatedly been an adulterer."

"My friends wanted me to make him suffer."

"My children just wanted it to go away."

"I cried for help from my In-law's, but they accused me of the adultery."

"I sought help or guidance from his male friends, all of them husbands of my closest friends. All they could say was: "You can't make him love you"; "Hang in there"; "We thought he would come to his senses."

You'll be mad, you'll scream, you'll cry, you'll think your attorney is not doing enough, you'll wonder why all the ugliness when you weren't the one that wanted the divorce in the first place? You'll think that since he left, at least he'll have the integrity to do the right things and show his children a good example in how he treats you now. That is delusional. As the Cher character said in the movie *Moonstruck*, "Snap out of it!"

Research the Family Law Code in your state, gather your data, see who will be willing to stand up for you if you need depositions, get a credit card in your name, stash some cash, love your children, hire a good and well-respected attorney, and become your own best friend. Find the inner strength to handle your affairs intelligently and lay the foundation for an acceptable new future. It's not the future you wanted, but you really do want to make it as good as possible. You are important. Your future is important.

See blog post:

http://suddenlysinglewomen.me/2012/06/11/can-you-grow-after-divorce/

3- Family Issues

How do you tell the family? Depending on your age, length of marriage, and age of your children (if any), the answer will vary. My children were twenty-seven and twenty-four during the year of the divorce. Is it easier on adult children than the younger ones? Not necessarily. Any age is going to have its own problems to deal with. Not only have you personally had to deal with the shock, now you're going to have to disturb the lives of others to make sure the truth gets out there.

See blog post:

http://suddenlysinglewomen.me/2012/04/30/shame-game/

The Children

I've had no formal training in child psychology other than twenty-one hours of psych courses in college. I do have plenty of years as a teacher and even more as a mom. But you don't need a psychologist to tell you things that are just plain common sense. No one escapes the hurt, the pain, and the disillusionment of divorce. Little ones wonder why their friends have two parents at home and they have only one. Even with shared custody, kids get unsettled being passed back and forth. Their favorite toy at one house, their favorite ball cap at the other.

Do we buy them duplicates of everything? That's just not feasible. Do they understand? No. Why should they? One day they're part of a family, one day they're not. Chances are high, unfortunately, that they've witnessed divorce and custody issues within their friend group already. Sadly, family units are out of vogue. It's been made so easy to divorce that few work hard enough to make marriage work.

We're a throwaway society. If people will not bother to recycle newspapers and plastic water bottles, can they be expected to go the extra mile to save the family? Evidently most feel their marriage is no longer worth it. People live more for themselves, and less for their children.

If your kids are adolescents, they'll put on the brave face but will wonder if the divorce is somehow their fault because they didn't make the sports team or didn't make good enough grades or played their music too loud.

Kids just want things to go back to the way they used to be, but they won't. They want dad to play catch with them outside, or mom to bring those cupcakes with the sprinkles to the classroom party. But now, instead of the schedules for all activities being on the fridge door with a magnet, they have to call and remind dad of the class recital, or they have to ask mom to be the one to oil up that baseball glove.

Teenagers can react with anger, shame, and fright. Not only has your world as you once knew it imploded, so has theirs. My guess is that they feel their disruptions are far worse than yours. They're not supposed to be the adult; you are. They trusted that until they spread their wings and left the nest that you "had their backs." They knew they could always count on you. Parents provide boundaries, stability. They make rules that teens love to hate, but also provide the underlying security that they are loved and protected. Now what?

When the kids had a problem, they used to be able to talk to mom and dad; now it's one or the other. If they tell one parent first, or pick one over the other as their confidant, do you hold it against them? Do you punish them somehow or sulk that you're no longer the "favorite" parent? It's like walking in a minefield. In a perfect world of no animosity, the family would all sit down together to discuss major decisions. They need to be able to look to you as the example of how to behave, how to act. You and your "ex" are still the parents.

Whether children are girls or boys will affect their response. Girls are appalled that dad has left. How could he do this? How could he leave my mom? Will my husband leave me someday, just because he can? Who's going to pay for my sixteenth birthday, my prom dress, my college, my wedding? They don't want to speak to him because he was supposed to be their knight in shining armor, the man they compare all boyfriends or future husbands to. Tears are shed, bubbles are burst and the fairy tale princess life is no more.

Boys are disgusted for a while. They don't shed public tears; they get mad. They are ready to fight. They question values that were taught and wonder why their father always preached integrity and the importance of a man's reputation when in reality their dad has just done the opposite.

The more you can simply leave the children out of it, the better. Did I? No, I didn't. Mostly I was always on the defensive from attacks and untruths being thrown at me from the opposing side. When those lies were told to my children, I felt the need to defend myself, such as proving with credit card statements that I had not run up a huge credit card debt. Was that a good idea? Who knows? Divorce presents so many situations in which you just don't know what the best choice is, even after the fact. Often, there simply isn't a good choice at all.

Try to find a common ground with your children because they are not pawns in a game. Respect that they have feelings and opinions. Remember Chapter 1 where I said no one can tell you how to feel? Kids come to their own conclusions and have feelings just as strong as yours.

It's no different with adult children. If they're already out of the house, they will most likely be even more shocked about a breakup. They were not around to see the dissolution of your marriage or witness the breakdown. Should you try to protect your children by never sharing their father's or your own failures? After all, if you decide not to divorce, their relationship with their father, or you, would never be damaged. You might think keeping it hidden is being pretty selfless; you think to grin and bear it is the best thing for them. Looking back, I'm still not sure if it was the right thing to do.

I believe in total honesty, and when you have adult children, they expect total honesty. Depending on the relationships either you or your husband has with them, someone needs to tell them what is really happening concerning the divorce. Doing it together would, once again, be ideal. No mudslinging or accusations would also be nice. Every family unit has different dynamics so you need to decide how best to approach your discussions with them.

See blog post:

http://suddenlysinglewomen.me/2013/03/06/the-great-debaters/

My husband separated from me over the phone. I have four good friends who each came home to find their husbands had moved out while they were either away or out of town. Another friend had her husband come home from work and tell her that he didn't love her anymore and that she should hire an attorney. You have no idea what's getting ready to happen to you, let alone what to say to your children who are gone from home at that time.

They won't want anger, accusations, and bitterness, but they'll want truth and they will need to know how're you're going to handle it. Do you have a plan, they'll ask? Can't you work it out, they question? Get ready for a flood of advice, be gracious, be receptive, but remind them that this is your life. All suggestions are generally meant to help, but it is still in your hands to make the decisions on how to move through this life change.

Often, the kids simply won't know how to respond, either immediately or for some time thereafter. My friend C.W. said,

> "Right after my husband moved out, my daughter said to me, 'Mom, why can't you be happy like Dad? He's moved on, why can't you?'
>
> That statement is hilarious, unless you are on the receiving end of it. Fortunately, with a little more time, maturity and insight, my daughter realizes how insensitive and ignorant that was."

As always, I believe it is vital that we make the best of a very difficult situation. Doing so will be a blessing to our children. My friend C.W. had this perspective:

As one of my good friends and fellow divorcees said, "Stay true to yourself and be consistent." Because, first and foremost, I am a mother of three adult children who look to me for normalcy, unconditional love, support, and grace. And I do know this, I am a better person now I am more grateful for the things I have, less judgmental, less material, less worried about what other people think, less inclined to meddle in my adult children's lives.

The In-Laws

Ah ... the in-laws! Somehow in our society the term "in-laws" has a bad connotation. I hope not in your case; it certainly wasn't in mine. I had the average family: a dad, a mom, one sibling, and myself. I married into a clan. I loved it. There were no shortages of aunts, uncles, cousins, siblings, nieces or nephews. We hosted family reunions every summer and exchanged Christmas cards, graduation announcements, wedding invitations and baby news. My children grew up knowing their grandparents as just an extension of the immediate family. Don't fool yourself that the divorce isn't just as hard on them as it is on your offspring.

My mother-in-law passed away just months before my husband walked away. I often sent up prayers of thanks that she didn't live to see his defection. She had married at nineteen and had three children, the first at age twenty. I was loved and accepted like a fourth child in her family. My sister-in-law called me her sister and I was proud of how close we all stayed even though we were sometimes separated by many states, once even an ocean!

When your spouse leaves, there is no rule about the in-laws. I thought after thirty years of marriage that the closeness we had shared would somehow remain the same, transcending the divorce. I'll remind you here that I've used the word *naïve* quite a lot when it comes to my thoughts and expectations post-divorce. With your indulgence, I'll use it once again. I was naïve. There's right, there's wrong, and then there's "blood!" I'm happy to say that I'm still very close to his mother's side of the family.

His mother's side (aunts, uncles, cousins, etc.) and I email, phone and, when travel permits, we see each other. They love me and have embraced me as a lifelong member of their immediate family. His siblings, though, no longer communicate with me, or reach out to me at all even though we've shared birthdays and Christmases and baptisms together. It's hurtful and makes you feel like a victim all over again. You'll need to get past this as best you can. While I am a proactive type person in my relationships, most people you know probably are not.

They don't want to make waves; they might feel that since your ex is the blood relation, they must distance themselves from you. Can you imagine what it feels like to take an eraser to the last twenty or thirty, maybe even forty years of your life as if those relationships never existed? I've heard cases where the ex is so domineering and controlling, you can understand why his family would make this choice. They are made to feel that they are betraying him, not to mention if there is a new wife in the mix now.

Friend's share that the ex's family overlook everything their ex did—a dangerous example to set for their children. Trying to convince them is a waste of time. Most friends who have shared with me their post-divorce situations and the family reactions to them have been the same. Everyone is far more comfortable moving on, and away from you.

You would hope that your ex's family maintains a relationship with your children throughout. It's certainly not the children's fault one parent walked away. My mother-in-law's family is evidently the exception, and not the rule. I am truly blessed and I say to them, thank you, I love you!

Always keep in mind though: it wasn't your ex's family who left you, it was just one person, one member of that family. Try never to hold it against them even though your feelings have been hurt. They just don't know how to act or what to do, so to them it's easier to do nothing. That doesn't make it right; it just makes it reality. Handling yourself now with good intentions and graciousness will answer for them (if they keep their eyes open) anything they've been questioning in the breakup of your marriage. That's easier said than done, but try your best to rise above.

I'm sad to say that recently my good friends Alice and Doug went through this with their son, who left his wife and three children. I told Doug I would be very disappointed in him if he did to his "soon to be" ex daughter-in-law what most in-laws are known to do. I am most happy to report that when the son got mad at his stepmother for remaining friends with his ex-wife, his dad told him to get over it, that he (the son) had divorced his wife, but they had not.

Way to go Doug!

4- The Friends

The topic of friends is what brought me around to the idea of forming a support group for divorcing, or divorced, women to begin with. Contemplating topics for such a group required research and a lot of idea sharing with my friends. I began to realize that if I was making a list of ideas and topics, I might as well organize them. Women started to ask me, "Why don't you put these ideas into a book? That is exactly the kind of resource that we need." So I did.

If you are still in the process of getting a divorce, you may or may not have come to this realization: your friendships will change. That never would have occurred to me. It typically doesn't. One woman, C.W. commented:

> "Things that blindsided me and knocked me off my feet? Well, everything blindsided me, but as an example: Some of my closest friends NOT taking my ex-husband's side, but not taking mine either. I have lost at least 3 friendships with a feeling of being dumped. I attribute it to the fact that these women were never really my friends and now feel threatened in their own marriages."

Of all the aspects of beginning life anew after divorce, losing friends was never something that crossed my radar screen. I used to think I was the luckiest woman in the world because of all the friendships I enjoyed. Some were friends that I had had as long as my thirty-year marriage. Many were friends I had met doing different good deeds within the world of community service and non-profits.

I had friends from the neighborhood, carpools, sports, and church. I am an equestrian, and my "Barn Buddies," as I called them, rode daily with me. We took riding lessons together and entered horse shows together. There were many friends from my time of service in the Houston Junior Forum. We called ourselves the "Renegades." I love needlepoint and through the previous twenty years had shared many good times with a wonderful group of lady friends who got together monthly to stitch. Once, some husbands suggested that we probably did more "bitching" than "stitching," so we became known as "Stitch and Bitch."

Wherever you look, no matter your walk of life, women enjoy a special kinship with each other. We laugh together, we cry together, we need our girlfriends like our lungs need air. They are there for you no matter what.

See blog post:

http://suddenlysinglewomem.me/2012/04/20/it-takes-a-village/

Men don't seem to want, or need, that kind of a "tell all" relationship with other men. They have friends at the office they might share lunch with, or the occasional hunting weekend. Men have their golf buddies, but rarely are the wives ever included in these male-bonding activities. Let me give you one woman's example of what can happen when you try to enter their world.

As LG related to me:

"My husband and I knew several couples that we spent most of our time with during those last years of our marriage. The wives had known each other first, but over time the husbands became good friends with each other as well. We were all very blessed with financial security and life's good fortunes. One important point to interject here is that my spouse and I were the only couple in this close group of friends still on our first marriage.

All these men had been married before, some more than once. Most of us had vacation homes, some in the mountains, some on the coast, but all within a stone's throw of a golf course. All the ladies golfed, or had taken it up to please their golfing spouses. Most of these second or third wives had never had children, and were ten to fifteen years younger than their spouses, but the same age as my husband and me (my husband was the youngest male in the group). From my vantage point, all the wives had husbands that totally adored them.

When we would travel together, all the husbands and wives played golf except me. Even though I was not at that time a golfer, however, I always rode along. I loved the outdoors, I loved the camaraderie, and as I said earlier, these women had been friends of mine first.

Because of my not playing golf, I came in for my share of ridicule from the group. Even though playful for the most part, they still admonished me for not taking up the game. So to put a stop to the ridicule, I finally did. I took private lessons, attended clinics, and bought all the accoutrements that go along with the sport: clubs, balls, shoes, clothes, visors, ball markers, more balls to replace the ones I would lose, turf pickers, tees, things to retrieve your balls from the water, things that measure your distance from the pin, books, more balls. I was going to become a golfer to make them proud, to make my husband proud, and to get them off my back so I wouldn't be fodder for cocktail-hour talk.

My mistake? Trying to please everyone else, believing they would love me more or think I was a better person or a better wife. In those last two years before the divorce, however, even after I had learned to play, not one of those friends, or even my spouse, ever asked me to play golf—not once. So I took matters into my own hands.

To surprise and please my husband, I arranged a weekend retreat at one of his favorite golf courses. I made the tee time, I had been practicing, and I so wanted him to be happy with me and proud of me. I would finally have him love me just like those other men did their golfing wives.

When we arrived there for our weekend, not only did he not seem to care about me playing golf with him, he invited along two of his men friends to join us. He then proceeded to tell me which holes I could play so it wouldn't slow them down. Wait a minute, I thought, wasn't this my tee time? Wouldn't this be my golf outing to make this man proud?

So my plan didn't work. My husband never did ask me to play golf. Neither did any of the golfing couples."

If you are going through a divorce, you are getting ready to learn who your true friends are. When you become a single, no longer a part of a couple, you become what I like to call the "inconvenient" friend. You are the third party at dinner, the eleventh person at a table of ten. No outing accommodates an odd number. At a restaurant, you either drag up a chair to the corner, or you have an empty chair beside you.

Couples that you saw on a regular basis beforehand now don't quite know what to do with you, so they do nothing. Hurtful? Yes. Fair? No.

The reality is that married women don't want single

women around their husbands. When someone told me that, I was so insulted. After all I'd been through, how could anyone worry about me sabotaging another person's marriage? I would never do that. Then I was forced to step back and remember that many times stories were shared by other women where it was *exactly* what had happened to them with the adulterous liaisons their husbands had formed.

In our social circle we had an older, single-woman friend who joined our group many times at restaurants, parties, and special events. I felt sorry for her and how lonely she must have been around us married people all the time. We made sure to include her. You can be blind to what is going on behind your back. Nevertheless, it was still very hard to think that after my own personal experience my women friends would be concerned that I would ever do that to them.

Once I became single, there were other dynamics at work as well. Women are curious; they ask questions, they gossip, they share stories, with full details both good and bad. Girlfriends want to comfort you. They'll sit on the sofa and hug you while you cry. They'll meet you for coffee or tea and listen while you each pour out your hearts to the other. They'll ask how you're doing, and they usually really want to know.

But sometimes you'll need to be careful, because some of them don't really care how you're doing. They're gathering information for tomorrow's lunch date with your mutual friends. These are the same girlfriends that will then turn around and say that they don't understand why you just can't "get over it?" They act concerned, say the right things, then go home to that adoring husband and promptly forget all about you. It can be hard to tell the difference. Are you now thinking and wondering who those real friends are, the ones that you can really count on?

See blog post:

http://suddenlysinglewomen.me/2012/03/09/when-they-just-dont-get-it/

Should you choose to share things with your girlfriends, just be very careful. They'll start to complain that they don't want to be around you anymore because you're full of anger, you're bitter, you're always so negative. What's really sad is that they are the very ones who bring it up! They are the one's asking you how you're doing! You can be asked but then ridiculed for actually answering. It doesn't seem fair, but it does work that way at times.

One of the most hurtful incidences of that

happening to me was at a restaurant one night with a very close friend I had known for twenty-five years. I knew she really cared about me, worried about me, and only wanted the very best for me. She knew I was having trouble wrapping up some final details what with divorcing, moving, etc. My friend asked how it was going, and I shared the lack of progress with her. At that point she said, "You know not everything is all about you all the time." You could have just slapped me. She was right of course; very little is about just me. But if she didn't want to hear what was happening, she shouldn't have asked.

Over time, my standard response to people became, "I'm getting there," "I'm working on it," and "I'm taking it one day at a time." That particular gal pal did that to me three more times before I'd finally had enough and told her I couldn't be around her anymore. We finally came to an agreement that when we "share," it was just that—a sharing of *our* personal feelings. We weren't asking how to be fixed, nor for advice, nor how we should handle our particular situation; we just need to say it out loud to someone.

How about your men friends? If you have any, most likely they're married to your closest lady friends. Through many years of my community involvement, I've had the good fortune to make friends with many wonderful and kind men.

There was the male friend banker who, before the divorce settlement was finalized or our family home sold, assured me that he would help me with a mortgage to buy a house on my own. I also had three men friends who took up for me with my husband when he walked out on me. One of them to this day invites me out to dinner on Valentine's Day with he and his wife.

Mostly the men thought my husband would "come to his senses." One told me to "Just hang in there!" Men friends will be honest with you. While for the most part women are the nurturers, men are the problem solvers. They're generally very honest and will tell you exactly what they think, foregoing the kid gloves. One of our closest male friends told me once, "You can't make him want you and you can't make him love you!"

One of the hardest pills to swallow is watching what was supposed to be *your* life, just carry on without your presence. This is a couples world, and your ex is going to have a new partner that enables him to still be a couple. Your couples friends will still do things with them; their justification will be "it's just about business." You will be on the outside looking in. Life carries on as if you'd never been in that picture at all.

See blog post:

http://suddenlysinglewomen.me/2012/09/30/the-optimist-creed/

Men will still do business with him. They will golf with him, they will play cards with him, they will fish or hunt with him, have lunch with him, play poker with him, just hang out and watch football with him. Maybe they don't agree with his actions, but they turn their heads and look the other way.

When I was younger, divorce was whispered about, but not many of my friends that I knew had divorced parents. These days, if the divorce rate is fifty percent, why are our children even getting married? So much is stacked against them. Added to that is the pain of emerging from divorce, only to find that the people that you trusted and loved as close friends just walk away because it is easier.

Surround yourself with people who think like you do and have similar interests and pursuits. Find a group of lady friends with the same belief system that you have, the same convictions as you, who make you laugh, and get you out of the house. You may just want to hide away from the world, but as hard as it is, put that smile on, don your favorite outfit and get out there.

See blog post:

http://suddenlysinglewomen.me/2017/03/06/same-song-second-verse/

Take the high road. You will find wonderful people to associate with who will value you as a person. Surround yourself with what you really adore. It can be your family and friends, pets, plants, special keepsakes with happy memories. Re-engage with your hobbies, music, reading, and crafts. Your home can be your best refuge to reconnect with who you are. You've been given a chance to start over, so go be the person you always wanted to be.

See blog post:

http://suddenlysinglewomen.me/2015/07/24/borrowed-from-a-friends-fb-postin/

and:

http://suddenlysinglewomen.me/2012/12/30/help-to-get-you-happy/

I believe in you. Believe in yourself!

5- Therapy

Divorces, and the aftermath, are grueling. We all need help to make it through in one piece (or should I say "peace"?). That help may come in the form of sitting in the office of a professional therapist and paying a lot of money to talk through the issues you are dealing with. But it doesn't have to take that form.

In the movie *Jerry Maguire*, the female lead lives at home with a cynical elder sister. Surrounded in many scenes by her sister's unhappy divorced female friends who are male bashing, the lead is the one who still believes in love.

When the first thoughts of starting a women-only, post-divorce self-help group took hold in my fertile brain, it was that group of women that I pictured in my head. I wanted to create a safe place where women could share together and support one another. But I wanted it to be a little more positive than the group in the movie!

For years I've had great women friends who would supply the opportunities we all needed to have a little free group therapy. One special friend, Anne, once said, "If we all were to throw our troubles into the middle of this table, most likely after seeing everyone else's we would chose to pick our own back up again." She was right. Our husbands thought all we did when we got together was bash men. Isn't that just like the male ego to think we all spend hours just talking about them?

In a group of girlfriends, mostly nothing is held back. Fine details are not necessary as we all get the picture. Do you have a group of girlfriends like I do, or like those in *Jerry Maguire*? How about the newer movie release, *It's Complicated*? That character's group was smaller, but the same principle applied—sharing with gal pals. We need to share. We receive great comfort in sharing, and many times the males in our lives are not comfortable sharing.

Don't underestimate the power of healing when you can share your innermost feelings with a group. Of course, as I said in the previous chapter, some friends won't want to hear how you feel. Leave them out of your inner circle. Surround yourself with those who can listen without judgment and who will hold your hand when you cry.

See blog post:

http://suddenlysinglewomen.me/2012/03/14/if-i-had-to-make-a-choice/

If you don't have a close circle of girlfriends but belong to a place of worship, talk with your pastor, priest or rabbi and see if perhaps there is a group within your faith where you can go for guidance and fellowship. Even if organized religion isn't your thing, you still might find meaningful support in a divorce recovery group that meets at a church (most of them do). Some such groups are overtly religious; others are much less so. I encourage you to check into what is available in your community. My passion is helping all women, no matter their religious preferences.

Books you can find at your library or online can help guide you through these tough times. One friend shared that when she was trying to recover from her husband's first affair, she went to her computer, logged onto Amazon, and ordered almost a dozen books on the subject so that she could begin the healing process. (Imagine her horror when she typed the word "Adultery" into the search and the first book that popped up was one written on how to *have* an affair.)

However, nothing can really replace you actually giving voice to your feelings and your hurts and your needs. Self-help can only take you so far. It's OK—necessary, even—to reach out and let someone, or some group, help you. When I'm looking for help on something I can't figure out on my own, there is a reason people say, "Google is your friend!" Look online for help or support groups, look in your local paper, ask your friends, even your attorney.

If you can afford it, and feel it's of value, seek guidance from a professional. These days there are so many well-trained and highly skilled people able to help. They have studied for years how to help people get to a happy and healthy place in their lives. Psychiatrists can prescribe medications if you both agree it's a necessary component for healing. Please don't think that you should be able to conquer this on your own. Your stress level, your anger or bitterness, your anxiety about your future can have a huge negative impact on your health.

There is nothing shameful in seeking professional guidance and counseling. These anxiety levels can cause you to lose sleep, lose or increase your appetite, and play havoc with your work, your concentration, and your ability to function normally. Your chest constricts, you can't breathe. Some women can't stop crying or find it difficult just to get out of bed in the morning. You learn to simply put one foot in front of the other, and live your life one day at a time.

I landed in the hospital with what we all thought was a heart attack. My blood pressure was off the charts. I couldn't breathe and the chest pains were crushing. It was horribly frightening to be hooked up to all those monitors and see the BP readings, and watch the erratic heartbeats. My youngest would not leave my side for forty-eight straight hours, spending the night in my hospital room, curling his 6'2" frame into a chair. You do not need to let it reach that level. Mine turned out to be a severe anxiety attack. You see, I thought I could deal with this alone, I could heal myself alone. I was wrong.

You can seek help from psychologists, psychotherapists, family therapists, life coaches and counselors, spiritual leaders—the list is endless.

Much like I advised with finding an attorney, search out a person that you feel comfortable with, who will let you voice your needs, and who does not make you feel silly, petty or insignificant. We are all individuals and, as such, should be treated as a person of value. If you are a square peg, don't let someone force you into the round hole. You are special, you are valuable, you are important. Good luck in finding someone, or some group, that agrees that you are.

See blog post starting with:

http://suddenlysinglewomen.me/2016/01/11/45-days-of-posit...ns-can-you-do-it/

6- Employment

Everyone's financial situation after divorce is different, but if you have not previously (or recently) been employed in a paying job, you will likely need to be. Alimony does not occur in every state, and even if it does, rarely is a single divorced woman's lifestyle ever going to remain the same as before. The working man's take-home income will take a hit with the divorce (if he has to pay alimony or child support), but day after day, post-divorce, it will continue to grow. Sadly, in most cases, yours will not. That's not fair, but it's reality. If you were a stay-at-home wife and/or mom, and you need to get back into the workforce, there are things that you will need to do to prepare.

First, you will need a resume. If you haven't worked in a long time, or were home raising your children, what do you list? Is being a homemaker something that has value in the workforce? Mothers can be the most organized "get things done" people in the world. Don't sell yourself short.

My guess is that you've done plenty of volunteer jobs in your school, neighborhood, church, Scouts, or kids' sports. You didn't just sit at home watching soap operas and preparing casseroles.

There are free services that can help you prepare a resume. Be concise. A one-page resume is what you need. Don't add a bunch of adjectives to the description of what you've accomplished; save that for an interview, where you'll have more time to expound on your qualifications and your desire to learn. Find past associations or jobs that you've had that show you can also think outside the box.

Mostly, just be honest about your situation and your desire to help your future employer reach his or her goals. You can be a team player, but also will not shirk your responsibilities of potential leadership. This process is a bit like dating. What is it about you that makes you different and desirable? What qualities do you have to show a potential employer that you are better, or more qualified than the next "date," or candidate?

Practice your interview with a friend, so that when you are in front of a recruiter or potential employer, you seem polished and sure of yourself. Sit up with good posture, look the interviewer in the eye and exude confidence. Don't look panicked or desperate, but do be honest at all times. Share your goals and how you think you can fit into their organization. The people doing the hiring talk to many candidates and are most likely very good at seeing through the "adjectives," so be sincere and place value on yourself.

Besides practicing how you will speak and conduct yourself, take that same care with your appearance. Everyone appreciates neat and clean. You have a mirror in your home; use it. Personal appearance tells a future employer a lot about how you feel about yourself, what kind of an employee you will be, and how you will work with others.

We all enjoy our freedom of expression, but a job interview is not the best place or time to display that. Of course it depends on the workplace you're hoping to become a part of. If you're going to be in an office, you're best to take a more conservative route in your dress. After you get the job, you can observe how coworkers dress on a daily basis. The interview process is not the time to express your personality via your wardrobe choices.

Do you need a new trim or a change in your hairstyle, or perhaps a whole new look for yourself? The large department stores have huge makeup counters full of products that they hope to sell you. However, it's also a wonderful place to go for a free makeup makeover without spending a fortune. Haven't we ladies learned that it's really more about the application technique than the actual product we use? Look at the magazine stands and find out what is current in the fashion world for your wardrobe and your face. Look at hairstyles that would be easy to replicate and maintain.

Nothing beats a really good haircut! If you've had long hair for a while, consider getting it cut off and get a new shorter, sassy style—it'll do wonders for your attitude. Can't afford a fancy salon haircut? Find a respected beauty school in your area and become the subject for a stylist in training. Do you need color? Please, oh please, don't go out looking for a job with those bad roots showing. Have gray? Consider covering it up to make you feel and look more youthful. Your resume won't lie about your age, however. If you are older, and your gray is natural and stylish—then I'm by no means advocating a switch to jet black. Your skin tone wouldn't exactly match. Use that mirror!

Never go heavy on the makeup. Leave the glitz and glamour for the evening. Be careful of the cut of your clothes, the length of your skirt, the height of your heels, the amount of jewelry and accessories. You've heard the old saying, "less is more"? What you wear to an interview is sending a message; let's be sure it's the message you want them to receive. Make sure the adornments to, and on, your body reflect how your future employer wishes to be represented. If you're applying for a job in a tattoo parlor, of course, that's a different game altogether. I'm just suggesting you dress the part for the job you're seeking.

Lastly, many people these days are looking for employment based on the company's available benefits. If your husband had a good job with good benefits, you lost out when he left. His employer may have helped pay health premiums. That will need to be replaced. Especially if you have children in your care, this can make or break your decision on where to work. Do your homework, and if you can't find the information you're seeking, ask. The state of healthcare in our country is frightening no matter what your personal politics may be.

Best case scenario, you will be able to negotiate to keep a COBRA policy that is paid for over the three years following the divorce (most COBRA policies last eighteen months). In a perfect world, after a marriage of 25+ years, I would like to see a provision in divorce settlements where your ex spouse will continue to pay your health insurance premiums until you qualify for Medicare. If you have not priced personal private health insurance yet, you are in for a shock.

Your post-divorce salary may not be in the same ballpark as your ex's, and your benefit package will most likely cost you more than his if he's part of a larger group plan. Review your options and be a smart consumer. One catastrophic illness could wipe you out. If you have children, most likely your ex can still cover them on his policy. If not, don't be afraid to ask a potential employer the appropriate questions so there won't be any surprises. You and your children deserve the best care available.

If your kids are not school age, you're going to have to find a childcare option that fits your needs, is convenient and certainly state certified. If you were a stay-at-home mom meeting their every need, do not feel guilty now that you cannot always be there for them. Children are amazingly resilient, and they won't be the only kids with a working mom. Make them part of the plan for "Mommy's" new life. They can help you do things in the home. Give them some responsibilities and hold them accountable. You will be doing them a big favor.

Have a family member, friend or neighbor as your back-up plan. Kids get sick, they get hurt, and there will be times when they need your attention. Knowing you have someone that could be available and cover for you if you aren't immediately available can be a blessing. I'm not male bashing when I say most likely your ex is not going to be the one you can count on. I will however, tell you of an instance that remains with me to this day.

I had a story shared with me about something that happened during an important meeting between a large corporate client, and their CPA firm. One of the corporate client's executives was a divorced single dad. During this client meeting, the school called to report that this executive's daughter had become ill and needed to be picked up at school. This man excused himself from this very important meeting between client and accounting firm and left to attend to his daughter's needs—with no apologies or guilt. My thought was "lucky girl," and my admiration grew for this man who was not embarrassed to do the right thing. Few of you, however, will be that fortunate, so find yourself a backup plan should you be unavailable at a moment in the future.

7- Finances and Budgets for the Present

Everyone's financial situation is going to be totally different, but as a woman on her own, it's so very important to know how to be financially savvy. In my case, I had been married for thirty years to a man who made all the financial decisions. When it came to money—anything having to do with household expenses, budgets and investments—he ruled the roost. Please never allow anyone to make you feel ill-equipped to make decisions when it comes to the family finances. Be involved and learn.

If that was ever the case that only men could make those savvy decisions about family finances, it's not so any more. We ladies are all smart enough to make sound financial decisions if given the right learning opportunities and the right tools with which to learn. In many households these days it's the wife and mother who handles the daily expenses of running the home. You do not need to be a "professional" to do it.

If you are in the process of getting a divorce, hopefully you've been able to get copies of your tax returns and any accounts that you share with your husband. Please note that I said "hopefully." After as many years of marriage as you have shared, do not make very bad and unwise assumptions that all your accounts were joint, and that both of your names were on all accounts.

Do yourself a favor and find out now. If you are in the throes of a divorce and there's any significant amount of cash and other assets, you would be wise to consider hiring a forensic accountant to make sure assets are not being hidden or secreted away. This is especially valuable if you are involved in a family business. Your attorney will be able to help you determine if this added expense is necessary. Every case is different.

All those promises of "I will take care of you, don't worry," now morph into "What you don't know about, I don't have to give you half of!" Separating men and their money is not an easy task, especially if you've been a stay-at-home mom. How many times has this been shared with me? All they can see is that *they* were the one getting up every day, going to work and bringing home a salary. When negotiating a divorce settlement, your value as a mom is diminished in their mind. You become the money-hungry piranha wanting something that you didn't earn and therefore are *not* entitled to! Don't stand for it!

At some point the divorce is finalized and you have a settlement. At this point (or, even better, before) you need to prepare an honest budget of living expenses. The first thing you need to do is make a list of all budget categories. This is *vital*. We jot down the budget items that are most obvious and forget the smaller items: highway tolls, parking fees, kids' haircuts, school supplies, soccer cleats, oil changes—the list is endless. Go online and print out a good budget sheet. The one on this page is great: DaveRamsey.com/category/tools.

Next, find out exactly how much you are spending in each category. You may have to estimate some things at first, but keep track of your actual expenses for at least a month to see how much you actually *do* spend.

Some of your spending habits will of necessity be different now. Divorce brings many life changes that will affect your budget. Do you have child support, alimony or just a flat settlement payout? Are you relocating? Should you rent or try to buy a house? Did you get COBRA insurance coverage for eighteen months (usually very expensive) or are you going to have to secure health insurance on your own? Do you need childcare, or a new vehicle to get to work? How is your wardrobe? Do the kids need new shoes, new clothes, school supplies, sports equipment, tuition payments?

How about all the utilities associated with owning a home? These days you have electricity, gas, water and sewer, trash, cable, internet, landline phone, and mobile phone, not to mention homeowner's or renter's insurance, auto insurance, life insurance, health insurance, groceries, doctor's bills, taxes. It never ends.

Look at all the current monthly payments you are incurring. Will you be moving into a smaller place? Will you have minor children living with you as the primary parent? How can you cut back on your expenses and still have a comfortable home? Utilities should drop with smaller square footage of living space, but children around can run those utilities right back up. Shop around for the best service providers and compare rates if you live in a big enough urban area to have choices.

If you need phone, Internet, and cable TV, look for providers that handle all and look for a package deal. Do your research and ask for the best deal, then ask for a better one! Can you live near work and use mass transit, or can you walk, ride a bike or carpool? How about where your children attend school or daycare—is there a bus, or a carpool, or a neighbor that can help get the kids to and fro?

If you need homeowner's insurance, renter's insurance, auto insurance, or life insurance, contact different agents to see if they offer discounts for covering all of your insurance needs. Did you know that the recommended minimum value amount of life insurance you should buy is ten times your gross income?

Remember when we talked about your job search and looking for good benefits? Good employee benefits will trim your costs substantially. How about food and grocery costs? It's expensive to feed a family and while you may be willing to get by with much less, your children need good nutrition for their days to be productive in school.

Is there a community garden nearby where you can trade gardening labor for produce? Do you live near a wholesale warehouse where you and your friends or neighbors can buy in bulk and split the packages up later between yourselves? For example, buy the package of thirty-two rolls of toilet paper and split it with three friends or neighbors. Buy three pounds of ground beef and re-wrap it into three one-pound portions that fit your recipe use. If you have any space in a yard, grow your own garden, or travel out of the city on weekends to a farmer's market with fresh produce and vegetables. In Houston, the farmer's markets come to us every weekend to sell their wares.

Look for home furnishings at resale and consignment shops or get creative with some sheets, fabric scraps, or slipcovers (more on this in Chapter 10). Haunt garage sales and flea markets and find used furniture that you can paint, or chairs that can have their seats recovered, or bookshelves you can put fabric or wallpaper around. Invest in a hot glue gun and turn your imagination loose!

Look for banks and credit cards that do not charge a service fee or annual fee (your local credit union is probably a great bet). You may be establishing credit in your own name for the first time, or maybe the first time in a very long time. Pay your bills on time and, if there is a problem, call your creditors. They need to hear from you. Financial advisors often suggest five percent as the maximum percentage of your take home pay that you should owe to credit card companies.

Setting up your new finances, as well as a new household, can be an overwhelming time of adjustment, but it can also be a source of joy and freedom from a negative past. You can find your pride again. So let's make an action plan for becoming your own financial boss!

1) **Find out how much you are spending.** As stated above, make a list of budget categories and track how much you spend in each.

2) **Make a realistic budget** based on your new spending needs and the money you have coming in or available.

See blog post:

http://suddenlysinglewomen.me/2016/08/23/have-a-plan/

3) **Put your financial goals in order** of priorities. What are the living expenses that you have to incur?

What kind of retirement account can you set up and participate in through your job or on your own? Do you have children that will need a college fund set up?

4) **Set aside emergency cash.** Emergencies always pop up that require cash: car repairs, home repairs, unexpected medical and dental bills, to say nothing of job loss or personal disability that prevents you from working for a while. Setting aside cash is the last thing that you'll want to do, of course. You need your cash right now, you'll think. Setting aside cash is never convenient, but you have to find a way to do it. Skip Starbucks, buy cheaper ice cream, forego that great pair of shoes you saw at the mall. Almost everyone can build a three- to six-month nest egg of cash (the recommended amount) if they work at it.

5) **Get some financial planning help.** Find a good financial planner or seek help from free public services to put your future needs in terms of good plan of action. What is a 401(K), what is an IRA, how do they work? It's suggested that you put aside 10% of your pretax income to save for retirement. Is that even possible starting out on your own with so many new expenses?

How do you have a balanced portfolio? What is the difference between stocks, bonds, mutual funds, treasury bills, and money markets? Find someone who speaks the language. One site recommended is FPAForFinancialPlanning.org. Others are: DailyWorth.com for smart tips and real-time money discussions with other women, or WomenAndCo.com for advice on budgeting, investments, careers and more.

Also see my blog post:

http://suddenlysinglewomen.me/2016/07/07/finances-you-gotta-have-a-plan/

6) **Get good tax advice.** You're taxes may be quite simple. If so, great. But make sure you aren't missing items you could claim as deductions. For that, you probably need an accountant or some good tax software (such as TurboTax). If you need an accountant, ask around for a referral. Make sure you are withholding enough from your paycheck. No one wants to be hit with a large tax bill at tax time. Now I set aside money every month and pay my taxes quarterly.

States have organizations for licensed accountants who may offer pro bono help. Call them and see how you can get help free or at reduced rates.

7) **Have good insurance coverage.** Find a good insurance agent who will be able to help you in all

phases of insurance. Remember, you may have health covered by your job, but you need auto, home (or renter's), life, possibly health or even long-term disability. A good site to check for names of good independent insurance agents is www.TrustedChoice.com. This site is operated by the Independent Insurance Agents and Brokers of America.

Use online tools to do some "comparison shopping" for medical and dental costs. Three reputable organizations are: HealthcareBlueBook.com, NewChoiceHealth.com and FairHealthConsumer.org. They list typical costs from providers for many medical procedures, and can also help with estimating costs you might have to pay with or without insurance coverage.

See blog post:

http://suddenlysinglewomen.me/2012/02/27/divorce-and-vanishing-healthcare/

8) **Get or refinance a good home loan**. If you want to buy a home and do not have an established relationship with your local bank or credit union, your other option is to shop for a home loan through a mortgage broker. They will be able to look at your situation and give you the best

recommendations on where to apply for a mortgage. They will be "shopper" for the best deal. A suggested website for this is www.NAMB.org. If you have a home loan, you will have to make sure it is in your name and check to see if you need to refinance. As of this writing, mortgage rates are very low

9) **Educate yourself.** I made some suggestions earlier in the chapter. Here are some more.

Take a basic personal finance class you can find online, through a local community college, or through a continuing education program offered at community centers. Join a women's investment club or money group. Looking in your local paper or go to www.MoneyClubs.com for one in your area.

Try reading one or all of these suggested books: *The Millionaire Next Door*, by Thomas J. Stanley and William D. Danko; *The Investment Answer*, by Daniel C. Goldie and Gordon S. Murray; *How to Make Your Money Last*, by Jane Bryant Quinn; and the *Charles Schwab's New Guide to Financial Independence*, by Charles Schwab.

Three useful websites I have found are: DownToEarthFinance.com, HouseLogic.com, and ShoppingNanny.com.

10) **Verify and establish good credit.** Check your credit reports to make sure everything is accurate and up to date. You're separating into two individual lives now, and his credit history may be more extensive than yours. Unless you kept your maiden name when you married, your credit history will be tied to his for a while. The three major credit bureaus are: Equifax at www.Equifax.com, Experian at www.Experian.com, and TransUnion at www.TransUnion.com. Without this information being current and correct, you will encounter issues in your financial future.

It might take a while for you to establish a healthy high score on your own, but be patient. After ten years of being divorced, my score has gone up over 100 points and I paid everything on time. That's exactly what creditors are looking for. It simply takes a while to establish a history of credit separately under your own name.

As suggested by the organization AARP, you can receive free or low-cost credit counseling and help with debt consolidation by calling the nonprofit National Foundation for Credit Counseling at: 800-388-2227. This organization if funded through monies raised from grants and donations and has an established network of community-based offices in every state. You can also go to their website at:

nfcc.org for advice and the necessary tools for learning to cope with debt.

♎

I went from being a daughter, to a wife, to a mother with no time for just being me. Many times you could be made to feel that handling of budgets, financial decisions and credit issues are simply beyond your mental capabilities. What your husband didn't handle, his CPA or your bookkeeper did.

Guess what—you *can* handle your finances. I can do it, too. I am doing it and am enjoying it. Being responsible for your own financial well-being empowers you and gives you a sense of accomplishment that no one can take away!

8- Financial Future

You've gotten through your divorce, you're managing your own life now, and your day-to-day expenses are (hopefully) under control. You're making good decisions with budgeting and how best to allocate your paycheck or your alimony. It looks like you'll be able to make it through the next twelve months—or at least to the next paycheck!

But what about the future? What about twenty years from now? Thirty? Forty? Do you have money set aside for your children's education, graduations, weddings—to say nothing of retirement?

The September 10, 2012 issue of *USA Today*

featured an article entitled "Get Financially Prepared Before Getting a Divorce." It may be too late for you to do exactly that, but it's not too late to prepare for your financial future. And the sooner you do so, starting today, the better.

Switching to a single income can be traumatizing. After 32 years of marriage, one woman, R.D., indicated her lifestyle changed dramatically after divorce:

"My biggest piece of advice is to know ahead of time what you'll face alone. You have to know what's ahead of you by yourself. I thought I was prepared, but you're never prepared enough to face financially what you'll go through."

This is *your* future now No one else is going to step up and take care of you. That may be a bummer, but it's the truth. I know I sound like a broken record, but if your husband handled all of the financial decisions when you were married, and you were never consulted concerning your wishes for your will, financial investments, or retirement plans, the future can sound daunting. Once your husband jumps ship, you have to do it all for yourself. Let's just say I wasn't prepared.

There are so many choices out there, and it can be

overwhelming—even to those who do understand it all. Who is going to advise you about Family Limited Partnerships, Master Limited Partnerships, Trusts, ByPass Trusts, and Marital Trusts? Or, if you're like I was, the simple difference between a traditional and a Roth IRA?

Yes, it can be difficult, and yes, it can be confusing, but this is your life. It's up to you to determine how comfortably you are going to be able to live. People live longer now and therefore can work longer. That means you will potentially have more years when you can save substantial amounts of money for future security. That's good, because does anyone really believe that Social Security and Medicare are going to take care of all their needs? We all need to be serious about good, long-term financial planning.

I know you didn't ask to be alone at this point in your life, and you certainly didn't ask to be placed in this situation financially, but here you are. The task may feel daunting, but it's not impossible by any means. All it really takes is educating yourself and getting some good advice. How do you start educating yourself? Start to familiarize yourself with financial and investing terminology. The financial section of the newspaper can get you started. Magazines like "Money" are better. These days, you can find most of what you need online. Go to the library or to Amazon and obtain one financial *Dummies* book. That should tell you most of what you need to know

Many investment firms put on seminars free to the public. Some businesses and churches have free sound financial advice offered by volunteers in that field wanting to help those in need. If you cannot afford to pay for it, do what you can to find these services through non-profits set up to help.

Are there friends or family members that you can trust to give you guidance? Use their wisdom. But make sure they actually do know what they are talking about. They may be most helpful by pointing you to professionals who can help you. If you have financial accounts of substantial size, you already have, or can easily get, professionals who can help you.

I do not recommend using the same people who have been you and your husband's financial advisors before. Start from scratch. Make sure, of course, that every financial account you have is now in your own name. If you were like some, almost all of them were in their husband's name.

The advisors you and your ex had will want to keep you as a client, but again, if you are like me, they dealt almost exclusively with my husband. I simply didn't think it was a good idea to open my entire financial life to advisors who were more loyal to him than to me. I found new advisors who welcomed my input, took the time to teach me the value of asking questions, and let me get involved in the financial planning for my own future.

Do your research on people, firms, the fees they charge and the services offered for those fees. Here are good two resources. For fee-only financial planners (who charge you by the hour), check out GarrettPlanningNetwork.com. On the other hand, if you want a planner who doesn't charge by the hour, but charges a retainer or a fee based on a percentage of assets, check out www.NAPFA.org.

If you have substantial debt, make a plan on how to handle it. In his book, *The Total Money Makeover*, financial expert Dave Ramsey offers advice on getting rid of debt. I recommend it. Ramsey presents a step-by-step plan, starting with cutting up your credit cards, writing a budget, and keeping aside allotments of cash in envelopes for things such as groceries, Christmas gifts, utilities, dining, etc. With patience and consistency you can become responsible for your finances and make informed decisions.

One final item. You'll need a new will. If you die, you don't want a judge making decisions for you in regard to your property and your heirs. Many banks have in- house specialists who can help you figure out your needs for a will, your investment strategies, and your long-term financial goals. Remember, it never hurts to ask for what help is available.

There are legal aid groups and firms that offer pro-bono services for those who cannot afford those sometimes costly and steep hourly rates of larger firm attorneys. Many women choose to write their simple wills with software packages bought online.

Remember: your finances are a vital part of your life. Be proactive. You are in charge now!

9- Education / Training

Did you give up your schooling to be a wife or a mother? Did you put a career goal on hold to support your husband's career? Was juggling babies, children, and family with a job too much and you stayed home? For women, this is a common story. Women, not men, primarily sacrifice all or part of their career for family. This is less so today, but is certainly still the case.

I'm a positive person who always tries to look for the silver lining in any situation, a person who views her glass as "half full" as opposed to "half empty." Yes—I'm one of those infuriating optimist types who always suggest looking at the bright side!

You can be too—really! Look at this new opportunity you've been granted. No, you didn't ask for it, but let's make the best of what you've been given. What did you want to be when you grew up? Did you have special dreams, far reaching goals, a vision of your future concerning which you hit the "pause" button on your remote control of life? Do you believe in second chances?

Can you see your way clear to trying, once again, to achieve your goal? There are limitless opportunities out there for a person willing to root them out. To start with, many colleges and universities offer continuing education classes for adults.

If you dropped out of high school, find out what it would take to get your GED. Did you drop out of college? Contact the college's registrar and get a copy of your transcript. You'd be amazed at how many hours could carry over even if it has been twenty, thirty or even forty years since you saw the inside of a classroom.

If you want to take college courses, you can begin by taking classes at a community college where timing and cost options may be more in line with what you're currently able to do. Meet with a guidance counselor who can translate your old credit hours into current class equivalents. If you want to start a new degree plan, they can help you. Many hours could be transferable.

There are day classes, night classes, weekend classes and classes online. If you have a bachelor's degree, see if getting an advanced degree is possible in your chosen field. If you want to study for a master's degree, check with your employer to see if the company covers any educational expenses. Pour over catalogs in your school, at your public library, or online for scholarship opportunities. Many just require an interview and/or an essay; you will never know until you do the research. There are thousands of scholarships out there; you just need to be diligent in your search.

How about your technical skills? Are they up to date? If you need to upgrade your computer skills, there are many classes offered around most cities for little or no cost. Again, your employer could pay for upgrading your tech skills. Some offer their own kind of scholarships, or perhaps financial aid, or even some kind of a work-study program where your training, or class work, is actually all part of your daily work regimen. If an employer invests time and money in training you, they are going to be plenty motivated to keep you around.

Not many jobs these days don't involve at least basic computer skills. If you do not own a computer, find a friend who has one, or a library that has one, and sit down and learn to use it. I was flabbergasted to learn that my 97-year-old mother had opened an email account. If she can do it, you can do it!

Work on your keyboard skills. If you'll be working with numbers, learn how to use the number keys without looking. Practice makes perfect. Speed and skill are still very important in the workplace. Software programs offer tutorials on the computer so familiarize yourself with the basics such as Microsoft Word, Microsoft Excel, PowerPoint, and Microsoft Outlook.

And remember, look on the bright side! Looking back five years from now, you will be amazed at the course your life has taken, if you smartly invest in yourself.

10- Home, Your Refuge

Are there times you just want to run away and hide? Believe me, I've been there. You get out when you have to, go to work, drop the kids at school, grocery shop because the night before you had breakfast cereal ... for dinner!

You're hurting, you're healing and you're hiding. At home you can lash out in anger, you can scream at the walls, you can cry alone in the dark. I'm not saying this is wrong; you're in a kind of twelve step program of your own, going through the post-traumatic stress of a divorce. The home you had made with your husband has been ripped away from you. Who is there to comfort you when you fall apart at night? No one. Your family grows tired of holding your hand, your friends grow weary of your "poor me, what am I going to do now?" routine. How long do you get to use the "get out of the self-pity jail free" card? Will it be a month, six months, a whole year?

Each divorced person's situation is different. The reaction over time of each person in your life will be different. A good number will probably come to the place where they expect you to "get over it" or "move on." When they do, and you're not yet over it, then you will feel … home alone. Even if all of your friends stay unbelievably supportive, you will *still* feel home alone.

See blog post:

http://suddenlysinglewomen.me/2013/10/07/putting-down-roo...like-a-water-oak/

So what do you do? You think you're not ready to go out all the time and be social yet. Then let's make your home a place of refuge! Let's make it your own personal sanctuary—your personal space where you are going to begin your new life. You're past life was occupied with making sure everyone else was comfy. You had a family home full of busyness. Remember when you used to beg for peace and quiet, some alone time? Well now that you have it, let's enjoy it.

Don't come home and think about all you've lost. Instead, think of all the independence you've gained. It's cliché to say it, buy hey, the remote control is now yours! You *are* in control. This is your home, so enjoy it. How about you try a quick little exercise to get yourself feeling better about no more "spouse in the house." I'll start you off with some possibles so you'll understand what I mean. Start off with a large pad of paper and a pen. Draw a line down the middle. Your category titles are: HE USED TO and SO NOW I GET TO.

HE USED TO	**SO NOW I GET TO**
• Hog the remote control	• Turn off the TV in the bedroom when it's time to go to bed
• Decide when we would leave an event	• Stay as long as I want if I'm having a really good time
• Leave the dirty towels hanging over the doors to dry	• Know the dirty towels are in the hamper out of sight
• Charge anything he wanted to buy on our credit cards, and then ask me, "How are we going to pay for this?"	• Buy without guilt if it's something I want *and* can afford
• Live on credit	• Pay cash, or only charge something I can pay off quickly, on time

• Drive too fast, roll through stop signs, make illegal turns, and cut in traffic	• Feel safer in my own vehicle and wait until it is my turn
• Arrive late and leave early	• Arrive on time out of politeness to my host and say "thank you" when I go
• Watch TV late with all the lights on	• Darken the room so I can fall asleep, and then fall asleep
• Want his dress shirts "just so," hand finished at only one particular cleaners, then make me return for a "re-do" when he was not pleased	• Go to any cleaners that does a nice job
• Tell everyone I never cooked when in fact the kids and I had already eaten at a normal dinner hour	• Fix a meal only once each evening
• Criticize my hair and make-up	• Skip the waterproof mascara since no one makes me cry anymore
• Try to make me dress like a Brooks Bros. business type	• Dress like the person that I am and enjoy the compliments of others
• Compare my occupation to his and find it lacking and "non-professional"	• Be proud of my teaching and volunteer jobs I've had—and know I've touched and changed lives
• Have to have the newest toys	• Love what I have instead of trying to have all I want

- Want to get from point A to point B with no stops or sunset
- Take the earliest flights back home to get back to "work"
- Wish there were no pets in the house … period
- Be angry all the time

- Stop and smell the roses, or watch a sunset, or take a leisurely stroll
- Take time to have a meal and leave afterward
- Enjoy snuggling with my own dog and foster others until adoption
- Smile when I wake up every morning without worrying what I'll do to irritate him today

OK, so I might have gotten a bit carried away in my example, but you see how much this can help? Try it and you might surprise yourself that being alone in your own home, living your own life might be something to look forward to. At worst, there are good and bad things about it. We are always better off if we focus on the good.

See blog post:

http://suddenlysinglewomen.me/2012/02/13/life-after-divorce/

So how can you make your home your refuge? Try thinking of your favorite things, what you like to do in your down time. Do you like to take a bubble bath and relax? Find scented candles to burn, buy one of those cushy spa pillows for your head, listen to soft and soothing sounds or your favorite music. If kids are still at home, put the "do not disturb or my Chihuahua will maul you" sign on the door!

See blog post:

http://suddenlysinglewomen.me/2012/05/11/a-playlist/

Do you like to read? How about finding a big comfy chair, a nice reading light and your favorite book? Use several really plump pillows at your back, under your arms and a soft, small blanket for your shoulders or your legs. You can even use earplugs to block out distracting sounds. Make sure that comfy chair or sofa is in a quiet little corner just for you. You can use a window seat or even your bed. Create your own private nook, not to read for work, or help kids with homework, but just for the pleasure of reading.

Do you enjoy cooking? Set aside an afternoon or an evening to just cook, cook, and cook to your heart's content. When you make something for dinner, why not double it and freeze a portion? Invite friends over for a communal supper. They can each have prep jobs, or each be responsible for their own dish. Share recipes with them, and they with you. Cook one big batch recipe, swap with three other families—you then have four nights of meals! Are there children in your home, or in the neighborhood? How about inviting them in to make sugar cut-out cookies with decorating icings and sprinkles that they can take home?

Do you sew? You can enjoy making something for yourself or as a gift. Buy discontinued print pillowcases and cut them down to make fun and inexpensive stuffed pillows. How about buying fabric scraps, or using old t-shirts or clothing items and making a quilt out of fabric squares? With straight seams you can buy discontinued fabrics, sheets, or coverlets and make curtains to sheer onto a rod for your windows or your outer shower curtain. You can also update chairs for your dining table by popping out the seat cushions, covering with the new fabric and using a staple gun to attach. Throw pretty sheer scarves over your lampshades to soften the look and the light.

Haunt resale shops and garage sales for little odds and ends to fix up your special place. Old furniture can be painted in fun colors to brighten up a spot in the house, a dark corner. Gather a group of old or cheap wooden photo frames and paint them all one color for a photo collage of family pictures for a blank wall. Start in the middle, leaving larger pieces for the outside, line up the bottoms of all the frames on the same horizontal line, and then work up and out. There's nothing better than surrounding yourself with photographic memories of happy times spent with loved ones, special friends, or memorable trips.

See blog post:

http://suddenlysinglewomen.me/2014/07/22/a-penny-saved/

Do you like to garden? Even if you're in an apartment with only a small patio or balcony, you can "container" garden. Buy old pots or containers at rummage sales, clean them up, spray paint them, sponge paint, and make them cheery. You can buy some flowering plants to put in them. In the winter, put in some plastic greenery bought at the craft store. How about growing things for the dinner table? Cherry tomatoes, or peppers, or even lettuces can grow in small places with sunlight.

Some ladies like handwork such as crewel, cross-stitch, needlepoint or knitting. If you have a project that you can start, it could relax you from your hectic day and give you something to watch developing, growing, and making progress as you create something by your own hands. Keep a nice tote or pretty wicker basket nearby so you can always pick it up and keep working. After all, this is now your home and you can leave your unfinished craft piece right where you want it! If you love crafts, find a fun project.

All those photos and clippings and tickets stubs you've been saving, now is the time to organize and catalog them into something special and meaningful that you can arrange in photo albums or scrapbooks. Make collages with spray adhesive to hang on the walls.

There are many "DIY" (Do It Yourself) shows on television and many magazines that can give you ideas on how to make your home your special place. Stroll through furniture store layouts; large department stores always have vignettes set up to draw your eye to different departments. They hire professionals to stage their displays to catch your attention, so *pay* attention. Be brave with color and paint an accent wall in your apartment or home. Many paint stores offer color wheels so that you can see what colors are popular and what shades complement each other.

You can stencil walls or use blue painter's tape to

cover your wall in stripes with an accent color or use wallpaper—which, of course, is a bit more permanent and needs wall prep. You can buy wooden fence pickets, trim them, paint them and use them as a headboard, or buy a pair of old shutters, paint them and hang them on the wall to create a fake window look.

Use mirrors to add light reflection and make any small space feel larger. Add rugs to the top of wood floors, tiled floors and even carpeted floors to add a splash of color, design, and comfort. Prop big, bold cushions against a wall corner to bring out for TV watching. Buy an old mismatched dish at a resale shop or garage sale and fill with mismatched sizes of candles in the same color to create a centerpiece for any table.

Baskets, baskets, and more baskets. Use them to hold books, magazines, children's toys, dog and cat toys, craft projects, TV remotes, pine cones, colored rocks or marbles, and Christmas tree balls. Do you collect anything? If so, find a special small table, shelf, fireplace mantel, or bar area to cluster your collection together.

Yes, decorating can be a dusting nightmare, but if it makes you smile it's worth it. Perhaps you get uneasy around clutter; maybe you think all of this is just junking up your home. If so, you can use those same baskets to "un-clutter" or organize your clutter. Put drawer organizers in your cabinets and group like items. Using a row of natural material baskets can keep your items in line. Put a photo on the outside of each basket so everyone knows which one to look in.

Buy colorful canisters with lids to store frequently-used items, from pasta in the pantry to cotton balls in the bathroom. If you use storage boxes to organize, buy colorful stacking ones and make them part of your house décor as footstools or side tables.

All of this is just to show you that being alone at home is not a bad thing.

See blog posts:

http://suddenlysinglewomen.me/2012/03/07/alone-again/

and:

http://suddenlysinglewomen.me/2012/03/11/lonely-vs-alone-8/

You can and you should make it *not* the place you hide, but the place you heal yourself. When you close the door at the end of the day, know that you will always be OK in your special space. Nothing can hurt you here unless you let it. Walk around and touch your favorite things. Make this a positive in your life; refuse to let anyone bring darkness or negative energy into your space. Until you're good for yourself, you won't be much good for anyone else.

See blog post:

http://suddenlysinglewomen.me/2013/10/24/who-deserves-it-more/

Below are listed some websites for perusing when it comes to home décor, both on a budget and simply for great ideas:

* CurtainWorks.com

* Ikea.com

*Lowes.com

* UrbanOutfitters.com

* WestElm.com

* Anthropologie.com

* CrateAndBarrel.com

* PotteryBarn.com

* RestorationHardware.com

* CalicoCorners.com

* HorChow.com

* LaylaGrace.com

* SmithAndNoble.com

* TheCurtainExchange.com

11-Fashion on a Budget

Every year my city has a large fundraiser benefiting the March of Dimes. It's a springtime luncheon and style show put on by Neiman Marcus and sponsored by the hometown newspaper. It's simply referred to as: "Best Dressed."

Past honorees can nominate people they consider to be (1) an outstanding philanthropist or a dedicated volunteer of long standing and (2) who exhibits a fashionable sense of style while out in the public eye. A closely guarded, secretive committee of the newspaper reviews the nominees and ten women are chosen each year. You may receiver this honor only three times, after which time you then enter the Best Dressed Hall of Fame. Many of those women have passed through my life at one time or another; I myself was nominated and received the honor once.

Does that necessarily mean I have good fashion sense? Not really. I would be less than honest if I didn't admit that I was surprised and excited when I got that call. All this is just my way of telling you that no one should have the power over you to make you feel you don't look good.

We all have our moments of wearing grubby clothes where we wouldn't be caught dead out in the public or run the risk of running into someone we might know I know I've had plenty of days where the workout clothes become the errand clothes, and then the carpool clothes. But that doesn't mean I don't know how to look good, does it?

See blog post:

http://suddenlysinglewomen.me/2016/03/17/what-not-to-wear...e-in-cheek-sorta/

Face it, we women are force fed what the designers and retailers think we should be wearing, and if you add on top of that the opinions of others and contests such as "Best Dressed," no wonder so many women have low self esteem, a bad body image and issues with fashion. Scanning the fashion magazines that tell you what to wear that particular season (which loosely translates into only "one" season) can make you want to burn everything in your closet and never leave the house.

They would like you to believe that the majority of women are a teeny size 2, 4 or 6, and that at a size 10, 12 or 14 you're beyond hope. Heaven forbid that you might even be larger? Want to know a secret? You are *not* too big. Go check out the sales rack in those designer-filled department stores and boutiques and tell me what sizes are left. All those 2's and 4's and a few 6's are still there, not your larger sizes, and you know why? We normal sized women have already made our purchases. Not many of those teeny 2's really exist out there in the real world.

Size doesn't make you happy, and designer duds don't make you a gracious woman. How you look on the outside should not determine how you feel on the inside. It's just the opposite. Fancy clothes don't make the woman. But we should all have things we can wear that simply make us smile. We feel we look good in them, and they are fun to wear.

Now I know what you're thinking, and I'm not

talking about your workout clothes, or your gardening clothes, or things you wear down at the beach or what you dress in to bake ten dozen cupcakes for the school carnival. I'm referring to what you wear when you step out of the house to go to work, to a charity meeting, to church, to meet friends for lunch—you get the picture.

You want to feel "put together" so that it's a boost to how you feel inside. When you're smiling inside you're going to have a happy glow on the outside. Somebody told me once that the compliment you seek is not, "Wow, what a great dress"; rather, the compliment you want is, "Wow, *you* look great!" The question is, how do we get there?

Not many people have an unlimited budget when it comes to fashion purchases, which also include the foundations, the shoes, the purses, the accessories, the jewelry—it's never ending. Men can get by with black shoes, black socks, white shirts, a navy suit, a dark grey suit, a few khakis and a sport coat. Have you ever tried to explain the "shoe thing" to a man? Do you see their eyes shutter like a garage door coming down? Enough said.

So how are we going to go about building a "stylish" wardrobe without spending money we don't have or don't need to be spending? One could write an entire book to answer that question, but let's at least cover a few basics. Your needs will vary, of course, depending on your age and your career demands, or if you stay at home. So have patience with me; remember, I only got "Best Dressed" once.

I researched and found the following list to be considered the "basics" and what to start out with. Here goes:

* Pencil Skirt

* Layering Tank Top

* Little Black Dress

* Perfect fitting boot-cut jeans in a dark wash

* Lightweight cardigan (neutral color)

* White pants

* Tote bag

* Ballet flats

* Black mid-heel pump

* Blazer jacket

* Black pants, skinny fit, straight to the ankle

After the basics, additional things to consider having

are:

* Menswear-inspired trousers

* Black flared pants

* Casual chinos

* Slim, ankle-length pants

* Dark tailored skirt

* Fun printed skirt

* Work worthy sheath dress

* Flirty sundress

* Casual cotton shift

* White button-down shirts (one cotton, one silky)

* Fitted tees (white, black and grey)

* Fitted tanks (white, black and grey)

* Long-sleeve striped tee

* Cardigan (colored)

* Flowery floral blouse

* Thin V-neck sweater for layering

* Tunic-length top or sweater

* Wool winter coat

* Lightweight jacket (like a trench coat)

* Menswear-inspired blazer

* Cropped jacket

* Flat leather sandals

* Flat boots (black or brown)

* Black heeled boots or booties

* Metallic evening shoes

I've run across many websites that you can look at for the pure pleasure of just looking. You don't have to join, or buy—it's window-shopping without leaving your home. Here are some of the ones you might enjoy, and heaven knows there are plenty more out there so have fun and explore:

* Coupons.com

* RedPlum.com

* RetailMeNot.com

* I-Ella.com

* Gilt.com

* LifeBooker.com

* IdeEli.com

* Groupon.com

* LivingSocial.com

Stores such as TJMaxx and Marshall's offer many reasonably priced clothes. Once you've fueled yourself with style ideas from magazines, web searches, or just people-watching, make yourself some notes of the basics that you will need to build a wardrobe. If your wardrobe funds are limited, stay away from more trendy items—you can always make your ensembles more fun by changing or adding belts, scarves, and accessories.

Do you live near any outlet malls where you can find super deals on classic pieces? One thing to be careful of: check the quality of workmanship put into the articles of clothing you try on. Check the seam allowances, the bindings, the zippers, the buttons, and any place where corners may have been cut to save costs. It does you no good to buy at a savings if it falls apart after the first wearing and washing. You don't want to have to pay for clothing repair (it's not cheap!).

If you have cable TV, numerous programs show women how to work with clothes they already own, or how to add pieces that can update your closet without having to start completely over. Of course we all have things in our closet that are just taking up space. There are "skinny clothes," the "fat clothes," the "what if" clothes or even in my closet the "boy, that would make a great costume the next time someone has a 50s-themed party" clothes.

As my mother-in-law used to lament, "Geez Louise"! Starting over after a divorce, especially if it involves a move, is a great time (here's my glass half-full attitude) to clean out and give yourself permission to start over. You hang onto clothes because they're sentimental or they cost so much money that you're going to fit back into them someday. Those pleated plants will come back into style someday; those shoulder pads will be back someday—not!

Get a friend you can trust and who will be brutally but kindly honest with you to come over and help you get rid of things. Try on, try on and try on some more. Start making piles. There are going to be some things that are "No way, Jose" going back into that closet. Fold them up and put them in a box to donate. *Do not open that box again*—promise me! Then you have the things that are classic, that fit well, that make you feel pretty, that are keepers. You can also make a pile that is the . . . well . . . maybes. Put those back in the closet, separate them from the keepers, and give yourself about a month to see 1) if you actually put them on to wear out, 2) if they really are worth keeping because they complement another outfit or 3) they're five pounds away from fitting!

I keep my closet obsessively organized. I hang things by season, and then by color. If I manage to put together a cute ensemble from separates, I write down that combination to remember. It's hard to go shopping for what you really need if you can't even remember what you already have. When you do shop, make a list of specific things that you need.

If you're trying to match or complement a specific color, take it with you—don't leave it to chance. Beware of impulse buying, or buying it because it's a steal. Until I was married to an accountant working at a very conservative firm, I never realized just how many shades of navy blue these manufacturers could come up with.

Even when you do take the item from your closet on your shopping expedition, and you think you've found the perfect match, drag your salesperson along with you to the closest window or exit door to see if it truly matches in natural light. You don't want to discover your new outfit is a mistake the minute you walk outside your house and realize that your colors are glaringly off. There's a good reason why experienced travelers work with basic black and add from there. Fluorescent lighting inside most retail stores is not your friend!

Fun places to shop include resale shops, consignments shops and vintage clothing boutiques. Some days you'll go in and find absolutely nothing, but on that rare occasion that you do, it's worth it. You can find some real treasures.

Don't forget to not only look at a piece for the piece itself, but also any adornments it might have that could be salvaged. For example, could beautiful buttons from an old worn out jacket or blazer add that "one of a kind" look to update a jacket you bought last year? Can you add a ribbon, a bow, a flower? What about changing belts on a jacket or a dress, or taking some old earrings and sew on as a brooch? Shorten a jacket's long sleeves to a three-quarter length with a cuff and funky buttons, or re-seam a men's tie to make a silk tie belt to put through waist loops on slacks or a skirt. Colorful scarves can be used so many different ways to add some zing to any monochromatic outfits you have. If nothing else, they make fun gift wrap for a present instead of paper to throw away!

12- Fitness and Self-Preservation

Are you taking good care of your physical self? Up to now, we've talked a lot about feelings we have and choices we are faced with, but you should never forget your body needs to be taken care of so that it can take care of you! If you are like most women, you focused on taking care of your husband's needs, then your children's needs, and your needs came last. It's time to take care of yourself, and your body's health. You only go around once in this life, so let's get healthy!

There are so many ways to keep your body healthy that one little chapter cannot do ample justice to any of them. What I'd like to do is give you things to consider, to research, to try until you find what's good for you as an individual. Do you have any idea how many things you can do in a workout with a simple hula-hoop? Blows the mind.

You probably have many friends that employ different routines for their fitness. Talk with them about what they find enjoyable and what works for them. Some may have a personal trainer, or a gym they use, or perhaps a home routine or certain pieces of workout equipment. Some fitness class instructors will allow people to bring a guest for a "trial" class that shouldn't cost as much as the regular one, if anything at all. It never hurts to ask.

Gyms offer trial memberships at a discount price, hoping, of course, that you will join. If you're employed full time, perhaps your company has a gym membership you could take advantage of? Many ladies take tennis shoes to work and walk distances to and from the car to the office or on their lunch hours. Have a long drive home through traffic? Walk an hour, let the traffic clear out, then head home.

I know not all jobs are conducive to scheduled workout classes, plus you might have timing issues with kids, schools and carpools. I know and I'm not saying those aren't important time demands—I've been there. But you are no good to them if you're not healthy yourself.

What kind of exercise do you prefer? We have to start somewhere, and sometimes something as easy as walking is the best way to begin. If you have just fifteen minutes you can give, you can try interval training in which you walk with a longer stride for three minutes, speed walk with swinging arms for two minutes, and then return to slower and longer strides, all the time breathing nice full breaths. Keep using bursts of energetic walking, or stairs perhaps, between regular walking.

Raising your cardio rate will burn more calories and help increase your endurance. If you use a treadmill, you can accomplish this by raising the incline. If you prefer being outdoors, you can walk a hilly area outside. Perhaps you want to integrate a little jogging with your walking, but not all ladies enjoy running. I'm one of them!

If you have any health issues or physical limitations, always speak with your doctor or an expert in fitness training before you try something new We can get overzealous and want to jump fully into a new routine, but that's never wise. Muscles that haven't been worked in a while will be tight and resistant and will not react well to your new determination. If you don't listen to your body, it will let you know fairly quickly that it's not happy with you!

Start slowly and build up to a routine that works for you. There are fitness magazines that show you workouts that can fit into your busy schedule. Stretches can be done before you even get out of bed every morning. For great ideas about getting back into a fitness routine, go online to RealSimple.com/quickfitness.

Working out and walking with a friend is always more motivational. The way we ladies like to visit, a thirty minute walk could feel like only ten minutes. No friend around when you need to work out? Then try an MP3 player with music geared to pump you up! I have found that I can burn more calories and go for longer stretches of time on my elliptical just by having great dance music on my iPod. You'll be amazed at the way the music can take over your rhythm or pace.

Explore what makes you feel good. It may be running, or it may be strength training with free weights, aerobics dance classes, Pilates, gyrotonics, gyrokinesis, tai chi, kickboxing—the list is endless. One will fit your lifestyle, and once you start you will begin to not only feel better, and look better, but also finally begin to feel in charge of your life again. When you look good, you feel good and conversely, when you feel good it shows and you look good.

A useful tool in my fitness program is wearing a FitBit. It tracks my daily steps and converts the total into distance and calorie burn. It also provides ways to connect online to monitor your sleep patterns and logs to input your calories eaten. If you have friends with FitBit, you can connect online to offer a little friendly competition—or motivation—to keep you moving.

See blog post:

http://suddenlysinglewomen.me/2015/03/02/walking-its-for-free/

I read recently of another resource, HealthRally.com, that allows you to set a fitness goal and invite friends and family to pledge financial and moral support. Meet the goal and the supporters could treat you to a spa day or a donation to your favorite charity!

The second part of the fitness equation is your diet. I use the word diet as a reference to what you eat and how you feed your body the fuel it needs to sustain itself, not as a reference to a weight-loss program. Stressors such as divorce are going to cause big changes in your body's ability to handle your diet. Some people quit eating and lose weight. For some women, food becomes their comfort and they eat too much and gain weight. I just want to concentrate here on a healthy diet. You know if you need to gain, lose, or just maintain. Nutrition is something that we all can agree we need to be cognizant of when talking about our body's health and fitness.

There are so many eating strategies out there these days, how on earth are we expected to know what's right for us? As long as you focus on basic nutrition and portion control, you can't go too far wrong. We're a country on overload and obsessed with model thinness and how we get "there" with our bodies. But we're not all born to be thin as a rail. Our DNA predetermines that some of our body types will not be that tall, that thin, that beautiful. When are we going to realize that we should be concerned with a person's inner beauty, not their outward appearance? Shouldn't our goals be more about being healthy, fit, happy and content?

Your diet is something that you can and should be in complete control of. A good start is assessing what you actually *do* eat. Keep a daily log of what you consume, both solids and liquids, each day for a week. I've done it, and it's an eye-opener. If you're experience is anything like mine, keeping track of what you're actually putting in your body will reveal this: you're consuming a lot of empty calories that (at best) aren't providing your body any nutritional value at all.

I encourage you to try it and examine the important nutritional aspects of your diet that you may be missing or ignoring completely. Some people, of course, have certain medical or allergy-based dietary limitations, but scientifically-based nutritional guidelines for food, vitamins and minerals can be a great beginning point for a healthier new you. For healthy food swaps and recipes, get AARP's *Eat This Not That! For a Longer, Leaner, Healthier Life* e-book at: AARP.org/EatThisNotThat.

A hurdle many (if not most) of us need to overcome in this regard is simple misinformation. A huge amount of new research has been conducted on diet and nutrition in the last couple of decades. Much of it contradicts what we were told to believe in the 1980s and 1990s. Some good, readable books have been coming out that summarize the latest findings. They are worth reading.

I recommend *Always Hungry?* by David Ludwig of Harvard Medical School. Among his main points: our bodies have certain nutritional needs and will, essentially, tell us to keep eating until we provide it what it needs. So if the calories we consume are empty, it will tell us to ... keep eating! Makes sense to me. If we focus on putting what we know are nutritional foods into our bodies, we can't go wrong.

Taking care of our bodies has an additional benefit. I know we've all heard the old saying, "The greatest revenge is looking good." It's true on so many levels, isn't it? A close friend said that to me once in front of my oldest son. He was appalled. As a male, perhaps he didn't understand the misery we women can put ourselves through if we are focused on trying to figure out what is wrong with us (which is what divorce causes most of us to do).

Taking good care of ourselves physically helps counteract our tendency to go down that path. There's very little that is wrong with us, ladies. It's just a sad fact in our society that men leave. Don't put all the blame on yourself, or begin to think less of yourself, your looks, your intelligence, and your sexuality. Doggone it, if looking good is going to make you feel better, then do it not for revenge, but do it for yourself. You deserve it. I deserve it; we all deserve it!

13- Outside Interests

Just as some of your girlfriends will help save you, so will keeping up with some outside interests. Do you have a hobby that you really enjoy? We've touched on this already when we talked about cooking, arts and crafts, sewing, reading, etc. Sometimes it can be really hard to think you're ever going to smile again, much less enjoy yourself while doing an activity.

If you have an old standby outside interest, try it again. Dig out those old painted needlepoint canvases or cross stitch projects. You might surprise yourself with how quickly it comes back. For me, since I was soon to be gaining a daughter-in-law, and all of my immediate family members had Christmas stockings that I had needlepointed, I wanted to make her one. I couldn't let her and my son's first Christmas together happen without a new stocking with her name on it!

That summer I searched and searched for the perfect canvas that would suit her and while I was vacationing in Colorado, I found it—a beautiful hand- painted stocking of an angel. It was so appropriate for the young lady who was such a loving and positive influence on my younger son during the dark days of the divorce. I was even able to use threads I already had with me and get started. It wasn't long before the creativity and joy of creating something so personal snuck in. I was smiling, thinking how surprised she'd be to see it hanging with mine and my sons'.

Do you have a passion in your life that can help you find your smile again? Let it be something that you do for yourself, for your own pleasure.

Maybe it's a more physical activity. Were you an actor "wanna be"? How about finding a small local theater group? Even if you don't get an acting part, how about helping with ticket sales, or backstage—just to be around it once again? Did you love reading, really submersing yourself in a good murder mystery or historical novel?

Were you good at entertaining and like being around people? Start doing it again. I used to love having people over. So after I got settled in my new place, sold the "marriage" pots and pans, and got rid of the "marriage" dishes that I'd used for thirty years, I bought some new ones and started cooking again.

So you're alone now, so am I, and so are more and more of our friends. I've discussed it before: no one really invites us out or over to their place, so we have to do it ourselves. One Friday night I had all singles over, men and women. Very few of them knew each other, but by the end of the evening it had been so much fun that some were offering to host the next one.

Yes, I cooked and no, it didn't have to be perfect. People just enjoy being around other people. They will always find something to talk about. You might even be surprised like I was when two guests I know from different areas of my life not only knew each other, but had daughters who were close friends—small world! What are the odds in a city of over five million people?

Depending on your employment status (and therefore the time you have available), there are always plenty of volunteer opportunities. You can deliver "meals on wheels" to the elderly or home-bound. If you enjoy kids, you can volunteer at your elementary school to read to the children once a week. If you love animals, how about offering to play with or walk the dogs at your local animal shelter? Talk about loyal and loving returns for your time spent!

In my city there is no shortage of charities or other organizations to become involved with. And there is no better way to lift your spirits and feel better about your circumstances than to give of your time. If you are working full time, how about organizing a toy drive for the holidays, or a clothing drive for people in need?

Get involved in your neighborhood with a food drive or recycling. Make it something you can all do together for the good of the community and make new friends along the way. Don't be deterred! I remember when my youngest was in high school and wanted to do a volunteer job of some sort. He contacted our church to help out with a Habitat for Humanity home build. Unfortunately, his available time didn't match the church's, and the church didn't help much to find him another opportunity.

But he was not to be deterred, and neither should you ever be. He ended up calling the local chapter of Habitat for Humanity directly, and found a project he could work on during his break time.

Everywhere you look there are 5K runs, 10Ks, marathons, and different groups holding fundraisers where you are can collect pledges from friends and family for every mile you walk or run as a donation to a particular charity. Now, one of my core beliefs is that the only living creatures meant to run were blessed at birth to have four legs, not two. Nevertheless, I could still find a way to raise funds!

Several years ago, one of the non-profits I serve on the board of became a registered beneficiary of the Chevron Houston Marathon. During the period of registration, the charity recruited runners to raise money for their cause. Not wanting to be left out, I devised a plan to help out—but not by running. I sent out emails to my friends to pay me to "stay in bed and steer clear of the streets" during the marathon's Sunday event.

One of my great friends and a *real* runner, Rufus, jokingly wrote back that he would be happy to sponsor my "virtual marathon" and from then on the name stuck. For years I sent out the request for donations benefiting my charity and got my friends and family to pay me not to run! As unbelievable as it may seem, I always made more in donations than the actual runners did!

All around there are races, bike rides, and walks, or just make it a personal challenge to yourself and get your friends, family and co-workers to pledge a certain amount to a favorite charity when you reach your goal. If you have any friends who have sons or daughters in Scouts, volunteer to be a leader or a helper to work with children. Help an Eagle Scout with a project to benefit a worthy organization. Collect food for your local food bank by setting up an office or neighborhood food drive.

We've touched on school volunteers for reading to children, but there are so very many other needs in the schools. Many will probably require you to have a background check, but that is understandable. You could cover phones for an hour so the receptionist can have lunch. Be a room monitor during the administration of standardized testing. Work as a school crossing guard or help the librarian re-shelve books.

Are you good at sports? There are teams that always need help with coaching, uniforms, snacks, drivers or manning the snack bars. How many times did I wonder if my little leaguers were going to survive during the season with the snack bar's offerings as dinner?

Make yourself feel good. Help others while helping yourself at the same time. It's a win-win all the way around. You will come out of it feeling so good that you've made a difference in the life of someone else, while helping to heal yourself. Accept the challenge and help make the world a better place for all of us.

See blog post:

http://suddenlysinglewomen.me/2015/10/22/mary-mary-quite-...your-garden-grow/

As a member of the national organization AARP, I receive newsletters with many interesting articles written with the older person in mind. That said, many of their ideas could apply to any age group. One list, called "Fun Is Where You Find It," caught my eye. I share with you some of their suggestions:

- Join a meet-up group where others share your interests, such as tennis, wine-tasting, bridge, ballroom dancing, book clubs and more. Find a group near you at www.MeetUp.com.

- Volunteer at a sporting event, festival, theater, museum or convention and get in on the fun free of charge.

- Visit local museums, zoos and gardens on the selected days when admission is free.

- Check out plays, concerts and sporting events at your local schools. They are free or low-cost and easy to get to.

- See a Broadway show or other arts productions at selected theaters that hold a lottery the day of the performance. Orchestra seats could be a bargain $25. You drop a card with your name in a bucket and an employee picks the winners.

- Get baseball tickets when senior discounts or half-price tickets are offered for designated games. As in live productions, no one wants to see empty seats. Deals are there to be had.

- Be serenaded by local entertainers at bars and restaurants—an inexpensive way to enjoy an evening!

14- Faith, Contentment, Inspiration, Spirituality & Motivation

It's been almost ten years since my divorce, and I can finally say I'm starting to "come out of it." When my eldest was around ten weeks old, he started to sleep through the night. So when child number two hit the ten-week mark, I foolishly assumed he too would begin to sleep through the night. He didn't. Lesson learned? You cannot predict life!

No one can say exactly when you'll realize that you

have "come out of it." We're all different. I was told once that it takes three to five years before you feel normal again, whole again. I read somewhere that if you take the total number years you were married and divide that number in half, that's your recovery time. Lord, I hoped not! I was married for thirty years; I didn't want my recovery to take fifteen years!

In the end, no one can tell you when you will feel better, or *how* to start feeling better. You will know *when* it happens; it's one of those "Ah Hah" moments in life. What's an "Ah Hah" moment? Well here's my example of one.

I came out of college with a "bucket list." I didn't wait till I was on the downhill side of life like the Jack Nicholson character in *The Bucket List* movie. Who knew I was ahead of my time? My bucket list was very simple (very simple considering it was 1975!) and was made up of five tangible goals. They weren't grand and glorious like achieving world peace or finding a cure for cancer. I decided they had to be 1) tangible and 2) achievable! They were:

- Attend the Kentucky Derby
- Attend Mardi Gras
- Travel to all fifty states

- Make a salary of $1,000 per month (remember I was a teacher!)

- Learn to ride horses English-style and to jump fences (on the horse, not by myself!)

So, back to the "Ah Hah" moment. While on a road trip one summer to hit some of the missing states on my fifty-state quest, I was crossing the border from Oregon into Idaho. To my left, on the north side of the highway, was a potato processing plant. The name on the property was . . . "Ore Ida"!

"Ah Hah!" I thought. "So *that's* why they're called Ore Ida frozen tater tots!"

I knew potatoes were grown in Idaho, but what I knew of Oregon had more to do with great Pinot Noir wines. Never had it occurred to me that the name of the potatoes had to do with the combination of the names of two states! It made me feel like I should have paid a bit more attention in geography, but still—now I knew

An "Ah Hah" moment is generally just as random as that. So when will your "Ah Hah" moment of divorce survival hit? I don't know - I truly wish I could give you the formula to get there as soon as humanly and emotionally possible, but I just can't.

No one can.

Remember how earlier in the book we discussed that divorce is like a death? The reality is that the life you once had is gone. That life has died; your marriage has died. It really is a death, so give yourself permission to grieve.

I also said at the beginning of the book that no one could tell you how you should feel. In the same way, no one can tell you how long to grieve. Obviously, if you are in serious emotional turmoil, your close friends and family are going to try to help you. It's important for you to let them.

A physical death has a permanency that offers closure, and grieving is expected and accepted. In divorce, the closure is not the same. For me much closure came on my court date when a few statements were read to me by an impartial judge who couldn't have cared less about my pain. I nodded my head and said I agreed to the terms of divorce. I signed the documents, the gavel fell, and I was lawfully a single person once again. The thirty years of my marriage melted away like wax on a candle.

That's exactly how you may feel in this process, like a mass of melted wax that nowhere near resembles the original candle. If so, that's perfectly understandable!

Jonathon Fields, author of *Uncertainty: Turning Fear and Doubt into Fuel for Brilliance*, is the founder of the Good Life Project, a movement designed to inspire people to live better. He suggests that we "embrace the chaos."

When things don't go as planned and we're not sure how they'll end, we tend to create doomsday scenarios. The uncertainty of a lost job becomes "I'll never work again." The pain of divorce becomes "I'll never be happy again." We see only the loss side of the equation, a phenomenon called *negativity bias*. As a safety mechanism, our brains are wired to go there automatically, but we can re-wire this impulse. Realize that there is rarely disruption without opportunity. Look for possibilities that arise from uncertainty and act on them. Ask yourself, "Where is the potential here? What doors have opened that once were closed? How can I turn this predicament into something extraordinary?"

Some of my friends have likened me to an old fashioned bobber on the end of a fishing pole line. You can try to tug me down under the water, but eventually I'm going to resurface and pop back up. We all don't have equal measures of that personality trait, but I believe all of us have an inner resilience that enables us to bounce back.

I am a Christian, and I believe in God as my Lord and Savior, but divorce doesn't care what your belief system is. I have dear friends who are Christian, Muslim, Jewish, etc., who have all faced divorce. They must all find personal meaning in their path of recovery. For the purpose of this book, I prefer to refer to it as spirituality. I believe we all find our spirituality in our own ways.

For me, I can find peace in watching the sunset and knowing I'm in the presence of miraculous things every day of my life. Music is spiritual to me. I can totally lose myself in music. Actually, I'm listening to my iPod Nano as I write this. My play list is made up of all the songs that make me smile, or feel good, or touch me in some way. They even put into words exactly how I feel on most days.

When I was first going through the struggles in our marital relationship, a very dear friend of mine, Patsy, mailed me a Martina McBride CD with a simple note attached. "Listen to song #13!" The song is "Bring on the Rain" and boy, did I feel like my life was in a downpour. Somehow this friend knew she could convey her concern, not through just words, but though the words of a song. I cannot tell you how many times I have listened to that one song to lift my spirits when life and my circumstances get me down.

What will it be for you? What will help you to make peace or come to grips with your situation? When will you be able to stand up and say, "Nothing's going to get me down?" It brings to mind the name of an old movie, *The Unsinkable Molly Brown*. You need to find your lifeline. Will it be your friends, your family, your faith? What will bring a sense of harmony back into your daily life?

Do you know why so many pediatricians have fish tanks in their waiting rooms? It's calming. Watching or listening to water is calming. There are DVD's and CD's of sounds and sights of nature. Can you sit and listen with your eyes closed and find a peaceful moment? What is your motivation to heal yourself and get back to being the wonderful, beautiful and glorious person that you are? We have to find out what motivates you to believe that you will survive this life-altering change. I truly believe that not only do we survive but also we end up being stronger and better women because of it.

Some people say that marriage is a 50/50 proposition. I'm sorry, but have you ever witnessed anyone who has that kind of marriage? Some say there's always two sides to every story and they would be right. However, just like there's no such thing as a truly 50/50 relationship, there's also no such thing as 50/50 blame for a failed marriage. There will be plenty of things you look back on; there's a reason they say hindsight is 20/20. I too had failures on my part in not always sharing my hurts, or listening to his. When did the line get crossed of no turning back?

Having said that, there's no point in endless rehashing in your own mind who was to blame for what in your marriage. I'm not perfect; no one is (how boring life would be if we all were perfect!). But assigning the blame percentage terms, like a stock market gain or loss, is a total waste of time. Doing that is looking in the rear view mirror.

During your divorce legal process, family and friends might encourage you to accept some of the earliest settlement offers. They want you to "move on" and get the divorce over with. You might feel they are rushing you about what you need to do legally, but they are right in the general sense about your needing to move on. There is no point in any of us dwelling on the past.

You must take care of yourself. Possibly for the first time in your life, you get to be the lead dog in your pack. I was first a daughter, then a wife, and then a mother. I was never just me. I always ate the metaphorical leftovers in my day-to-day life. Don't get me wrong—I was happy doing it. As a woman, being a combination of Southern and Texan makes me the eternal "pleaser" to everyone around me. I was very good at that job, too. I learned from the best—my mother!

During the divorce process, I had to turn the people pleaser off and make tough decisions. That started with the legal process. Depending on your own personal situation, you will simply find it amazing to hear what your spouse is saying about your marriage and you personally. None of those things matter in the least, true or not, if you allow them to distract you, or hurt you.

Do what you need to do to defend yourself legally against false accusations, and then move on. It is a *supreme* waste of your time to answer his accusations or defend yourself to him personally. What we have to face is that our former spouse is already gone from the relationship. He was, and is, emotionally unavailable. There was not, and never was, a way to save the marriage. To him, you are a business deal gone badly, and the sooner you can close that door, the sooner you are on your way to recovery.

The day may come when you have to take additional legal action after the divorce. If you have to file what's called an Enforcement Order, be prepared that those actions will be seen as anger. In reality, it is a breach of contract. You will do yourself a huge disservice to think that everyone you care about is going to agree with your every move. At the end of the day you and you alone are accountable for your actions. Life is never easy, and it certainly is not as cut and dried as your family, or friends, or you hoped it would be.

From everyone else's perspective, there is no right or wrong in a divorce. It's just another marriage failure. People don't care about the details and they're ready to move on from your tale of woe. Whatever blame you can assess and reasons you can provide them will never repair your heart. Finding the sutures needed to repair your heart is completely up to you. A few good friends or family members may help, but they can't do it for you.

Whether you find your solace and healing in friendships, in therapy, in new directions you choose to take, or in your spirituality, the motivation to get there is up to you, and you alone. These may be tough words to hear, especially if you have not fully embraced this reality for yourself yet. But just think how proud you'll be when you start down that path of recovery.

As you do, it is vital remember this: you are not alone. You have not been alone in what has happened and you are not alone in what will happen from here. Others *will* be there for you. The darkness of night will sometimes press in on your life like a five-ton elephant, but the dawn will come and you'll have a chance to make yourself whole once again.

15- Dating

This is a tough one. I almost didn't put this chapter in because it's beyond personal! But eventually, the thought of going out on a date may cross your mind. So ...

Offering her marriage therapist's advice, HB shared:

"After my husband's affair came to light, we decided we should go to a marriage counselor to "repair the hurt" from the infidelity and save the marriage. Eventually, like my husband's other promises and best intentions, the sessions were stopped. However, one of the things that stuck with me from those sessions was a statement made by the therapist.

Basically what he said was most men don't leave their wives, their marriage, their children or the history made within the marriage. That history you have together is just too great and irreplaceable. (You might feel like the exceptions to that rule!) He then followed up that statement with *his* exception to the rule.

Men that do leave do so with another woman already in place. In other words, men don't do "alone." That was certainly true in my case. Of course, my husband convinced his family, regardless of the email, cell phone and photographic evidence to the contrary, that he started that relationship with her after our separation/divorce. As kids these days say, "Whatever!" My spouse was dating *while* married; of course he would continue to do it while separated.

The thought of dating was so far down on my list of "to do's" in that first year that I scoffed at the idea of ever letting any male close enough to have the power to hurt me again. Talk about being burned! No way Jose! I've spent many an interesting evening with single women who have no desire to ever subject themselves to the whims or controls of another man."

After hearing that, it made me wonder. Bitter feelings, you say? No, not really. These women are just very, very comfortable with being on their own. Either their children, or their careers, or their life's passions are more than enough to make them whole.

Not so for me.

Don't mistake my meaning. I am completely self-sufficient and I adore my children and enjoy my life's passions. I just happen to want to enjoy sharing my life with (for lack of a better description) a "life" partner! And the only way to find one is through getting yourself out there and dating.

See blog post:

http://suddenlysinglewomen.me/2014/08/15/a-humorous-list-for-dating-rules/

In writing this chapter I'm going to assume that you are closer to my age than you are to your age at your high school graduation. If so, welcome to the new world of dating. If not, read on and at least benefit from the wisdom of someone from your mother's generation!

It's shocking how much dating has changed in the thirty-plus years since I married. It's hard to enter a world of internet dating sites, cell phones, Facebook, web cams—and to think I used to dread those fraternity match date events while in college! That "dates" me for sure! Nor could I do what women of an earlier era may have done and just walk into a bar and wait for Mr. Right to show up. I'm not a bar fly, and in any case, trust me that the single men trolling for women at bars are not looking in our age range.

When I think of blind dates at our age, the term "blind" may have shifted back to its original meaning! Heaven help me, but I need some humor to make this process more palatable. I get through it by nicknaming my dates to bring that levity into it—after all, it's better than running away and screaming.

When your friends set you up with a given gentleman, you begin to question what exactly your friends think of you. When I go on such arranged dates, I think, what part of me did my friends think would be a good match with this person?

I tried going to singles parties with friends at their churches. A great way to meet other singles—if you're a man! I'd say the ratio of females to males at these events was about ten to one.

What about online dating? After the

mega-bestselling book *The Da Vinci Code* was released a number of years back, an expert on religious manuscripts from the first few centuries A.D. (on which the book's premise relied) was asked how much of what the book claimed was actually true. He replied, "Well, Paris is an actual city, and Da Vinci was an actual painter. That's about it."

That's kind of the way I feel about online dating. It is online, and it is about dating—sort of. Do people find their match made in heaven through online dating? Probably. I'm just not sure who any of them are.

Not that long ago, after a hiatus, I decided to give online dating another try. I signed up, interacted with some men online, and arranged for a number of "meet and greets." I met the first at a restaurant where we sat at the bar drinking iced tea (I think most men have decided that treating women they meet online to an actual dinner is far too large an investment). After chatting for two hours, he had to leave for a business meeting, saying he would love to continue over dinner. I never heard from him again, except he did send a "like" via the dating website, saying I seemed like a person he'd like to meet. What? We already met, you bozo!

The second meet and greet was with a very nice

retired gentleman who showed me photos of all the guest bedrooms in his country home. You've heard of young people with an old soul? This was an old person with an old soul. I think he realized I was a bit too active for him.

Number three had an actual dinner with me and we talked for three and a half hours. He says he'd love to take me out dancing next time. I never heard from him about a next time. A year later, I get a "like" from him and I had to remind him we'd already met before. BIG SIGH!

Number four suggested we meet at a restaurant near both of us on a Tuesday evening at 7:00. Meeting at a restaurant at 7:00 implied dinner to me, but I was wrong. I sat down at a booth and he remained standing for a time. Standing! He finally treated me to a glass of lemonade. He got water. After an hour, I excused myself to head back home. I emailed him the next morning, thanked him for my "lemonade" and told him I didn't think there was a connection between us. He emailed back: "Wow, I'm reading your email and wondering what happened to the woman I met last night? No connection? That's not what your body language was saying!" Maybe I needed to check what language my body was speaking?

Number five had so many good qualities and we had such a good start via cyber space … for two days. Didn't hear from him after that. With number six, we almost got to the point of setting up a get-together, and then he emailed saying he reread my profile and he just couldn't see a woman who loves horses. What?

I never even communicated with number seven. He just sent me an unsolicited comment: "Wow. All you have is pictures of your family, dogs, horses, babies, and group pictures of your friends. Just so you know, men want to see just you—they could care less about seeing dogs and horses and all that junk—it totally turned me away. (I know being honest will piss you off—but someone should tell you.)" Seriously? Thanks for the input.

I haven't given up on the possibility of meeting someone online. Neither have many of my friends. We've just concluded that in the evening activity competition between online dating and Netflix, Netflix wins, hands down.

(For more stories, adventures, and yes, actual advice about the topics covered in this book, I invite you to follow my blog at:

SuddenlySingleWomen.Wordpress.com.

As I said before, it's a couple's world and the only way to get back into that world is to find yourself an escort (no, not *that* kind of escort). I attend functions for many of the non-profits I volunteer for and am always in need of a nice gentleman escort. But you end up paying for the evening, trying to make sure he meets your friends and is comfortable, and you wonder if it's really worth it.

You meet men who are divorced themselves, or widowers, and you end up being compared to their ex or not able to live up to the memory of someone who's passed away.

Men seem to be able to get invited to parties and dinners and social occasions without a date and appear normal, comfortable and fully at ease. Single women? Not so much. You're either a threat or inconvenient, so dating becomes not only a matter of fighting off loneliness, but being able to go out and do things that you were used to doing in your married life.

So there will be some nights that you sit on your sofa watching another TV program or eating another lonely meal and you throw yourself the occasional pity party. Been there! Your friends tell you, "It'll happen when you quit trying to make it happen!" Really? If you're lucky enough to find a nice companion and begin to spend time with him, good for you. But this doesn't even touch on the humiliating thought of having to get intimate with someone new for the first time in years. Shudder!

One friend, A.R., contributed these thoughts on getting "out there":

"What I did right after the divorce is I promise myself I would never sit home alone on a Friday or Saturday night. I went out and bought new clothes, got new makeup, and signed up for a dating service so I could have one date a month.

I joined some singles groups, joined a divorce recovery group, and made new girlfriends because I lost a lot of girlfriends in the divorce. I kept my promise to myself to make sure at the beginning of each week I was setting up events for the weekend because I found out that calling people after Wednesday was too late. The pain, fear and terror were with me during the week but not on Friday or Saturday night. Getting out and meeting people were activities I think saved my life."

See blog post:

http://suddenlysinglewomen.me/2012/02/25/its-the-weekend-yay-or-boo/

The best I can say to you is just to take your time, don't rush anything, and be safe. There are some really strange people out there and we have to be very careful trusting again. The rules have changed, the timing has changed, the diseases have changed—it's not fair, but it's reality. However you decide to start meeting people, and whenever you decide to start dating again, be patient with yourself and stay true to yourself. And most importantly, love yourself. You deserve it.

See blog post:

http://suddenlysinglewomen.me/2012/03/04/dating-after-divorce-7-2/

I'll end with a quote I came across that both gives hope and brilliantly describes the process you are going through:

"And the day came, when the risk to remain tight in a bud was more painful than the risk it took to blossom."

As you blossom, may your petals shine more brightly than ever before. You can do it!

About The Author
Lynda Lighthouse Transier

Lynda Transier is a native Houstonian, a graduate of Milby High School and the University of Texas where she received the dual degree of Bachelors of Science in Elementary Education/Special Education with a minor in Psychology. She is the mother of two. After spending eight years as a Special Education/Reading Specialist teacher, first at Austin State School, then in Spring Branch ISD, she became a full-time mother and volunteer.

She has chaired events for the Houston Junior Forum, Texas Society of CPAs, Zoo Ball, Child Advocates, Houston Ballet, Juvenile Diabetes, Nutcracker Market, Cattle Baron's Ball, Escape Family Resources, March of Dimes, the International Committee for the Houston Livestock Show and Rodeo, Easter Seals, Friends For Life, Houston's only No Kill Animal Shelter, and the Family Services of Houston 100th Anniversary Gala in February 2004. She co-chaired the Houston Audubon Society Gala. Honors received include NSFRE Volunteer of the Year – 1994, Friends of

Child Advocates Luncheon Honoree – 1998, Woman of Distinction – 1998, I Have a Dream Family of the Year – 2001, Houston Pacesetter Award – 2001, Hats Off to Mother's Honoree – 2002 and Houston Chronicle Best Dressed – 2002. Monies raised from events Lynda has chaired exceed four million dollars.

Lynda has or currently serves on the Boards of the Houston Ballet Foundation, Cynthia Woods Mitchell Pavilion, I Have a Dream – Houston, Pin Oak Charity Horse Show, Hospice at the Texas Medical Center, Houston Arts Alliance, Theatre Under the Stars/TUTS, Child Advocates, Inc., and the Advisory Boards of Girls, Inc., Dress for Success – Houston and VICTORY/American Cancer Society. She also was a working member on the capital campaigns of the River Oaks Baptist School, Girl Scouts – San Jacinto Council, Houston Ballet Foundation and TUTS.

Lynda enjoys spending time with her two children, their spouses and her grandchildren, planning special events, summer retreats to Colorado, needlepoint and riding her horses. She adopted two rescue German Shepherds, Sascha and Blanco and fosters for the Greater Houston German Shepherd Dog Rescue.

Register this BOOK!

Register your book and you will receive a free "What to ask your attorney" divorce guide along with updates to this book, access to more information, and access to our blog that help you ALONG YOUR JOURNEY.

Just visit: www.SuddenlySingleWomen.info

For more stories, adventures, and advice about the topics covered in this book, I invite you to follow my blog at SuddenlySingleWomen.Wordpress.com.

Made in the USA
Columbia, SC
04 March 2023

13321694R00100